STEPHANIE

STEPHANIE

A Girl in a Million

STEPHANIE ANNE LLOYD

with Sandra Sedgbeer

EBURY PRESS
London

Dedication

*To those I have loved and lost
and those I have found and love*

Published in 1991 by Ebury Press
an imprint of the Random Century Group
Random Century House
20 Vauxhall Bridge Road
London SW1V 2SA

British Library Cataloguing in Publication Data
Lloyd, Stephanie Ann
Stephanie.
1. Transsexualism. Biographies
I. Title   II. Sedgbeer, Sandra

ISBN 0-85223-927-0

Printed and bound in Great Britain by
Mackays of Chatham Plc, Kent

Filmset in Baskerville by Advanced Filmsetters (Glasgow) Ltd, Glasgow

CONTENTS

Introduction   6

Prologue   7

KEITH

1 The Early Years   11
2 Becoming A Man   27
3 Missionary Zeal   41
4 First Love   57
5 Snakes and Ladders   71
6 Rock Bottom   85

STEPHANIE

7 Born Again   105
8 Transformation   121
9 Unusual Services   138
10 Last Love   156
11 The Phoenix Rises   168
12 Reflections   183

INTRODUCTION

I have long been a keen reader of autobiographies and have never before thought to question the exemplary lives the authors seem to have led. It was only when I came to write my own autobiography that I discovered the almost overwhelming compulsion to omit all of the parts one is ashamed of, or to censor the mistakes and errors that, with hindsight, reflect badly on one. We all have a natural tendency to gloss over the darker aspects of ourselves as well as those unhappy circumstances that are of our own making – yet writing an autobiography inevitably creates a dilemma: not only have I been forced to relive my life, but also to lay that life bare for public consumption and, possibly, even condemnation!

It has been extremely difficult to produce, but here you have a painfully *honest* account of my life. The story you are about to read traces my life in excruciating detail. In forcing myself to record all of my mistakes, I have relived the torment and endured the pain of incidents that reflect my inadequacies and thoughtlessness.

Yet nothing can undo the past and no one, I am sure, could judge me more harshly than I have judged myself. And so, as my story unfolds, I would ask you to remember that my increasingly inexplicable, irrational and sometimes outrageous behaviour was a confused and emotionally unstable person's reaction to a problem of sexual identity that was growing ever larger and more terrifying with each passing year.

My fervent prayer is that this book will help my beloved parents, my beautiful and loving ex-wife and my three irreplaceable children truly to understand the complex and wholly untenable condition that I fought to come to terms with. I hope that they will find a way to forgive me, and that some time in the future we will all find a way of salvaging a new and lasting relationship out of the overwhelming disaster that overtook us all. If, in addition, my story serves to educate, to help minimize the mystery and prejudice that surrounds transsexualism and provide some solace to those unfortunate few who are forced to follow in my footsteps, then I will count this a bonus.

PROLOGUE
September 1983

As I undressed and changed into my hospital gown, I tried to avoid catching sight of myself in the mirror that stretched the entire width of the wall. I couldn't bear to look at my body and see the evidence of what I had become – an in-betweeny, with the full, firm breasts of a woman and the genitals of a man. I felt, and looked, a freak. That thought alone was enough to make me realize that tomorrow couldn't arrive soon enough.

Was it really only twelve hours since I'd left my house to embark upon what I could only describe as the greatest journey of my life? It seemed like years ago. My memories of the taxi journey to the airport, the brief flight to London and my underground ride to Hammersmith Station were hazy; I'd been far too preoccupied with my own thoughts to take much notice of what had been going on around me as I had journeyed south to London for my appointment with my future – if, indeed, I was to have a future, I mentally amended.

The staff here at the Charing Cross Hospital had been wonderful as they had taken me through the normal admittance procedure before showing me to my room. Of course they knew who – and what – I was, but they were far too professional to display any prurient interest.

Now, at long last, all the necessary first day formalities had been taken care of and I was alone in my hospital bed with just my thoughts for company. Soon, one of the night staff would come in to offer me the obligatory little white pill that would provide a merciful night's oblivion – though why they thought I should need a good night's sleep, when I would be spending the next few days heavily sedated, I couldn't quite work out. I hoped they wouldn't come too soon, for I needed these few precious moments of solitude to sort out my conflicting emotions. It wasn't that I had any doubts about my decision, for those had all been resolved a long time ago. I simply knew that, before I could face the future, I had to come to terms with the past.

Tears slid slowly down my face as I recalled the hurt and pain

7

I had inflicted on others in the years during which I had selfishly avoided coming to terms with my condition. If only I had known that, no matter how I tried to fight the truth, I'd still end up in this hospital bed facing the most dramatic moment of my life! Perhaps then I would have been better equipped to spare so many people the anguish I had unwittingly subjected them to. But here I was, and nothing, not all the regrets in the world, could change the past. All I could do was try and change my future. After all, wasn't that the very reason I was here?

Despite my Jehovah's Witness upbringing I had never been particularly religious, but I *did* believe in God. And right then I felt a compelling need to pray. Though many people might think that wrong, I felt as though I needed someone to talk to, someone to explain myself to who might perhaps forgive me for what I was about to do.

'Please, God,' I prayed, 'help my parents and family to understand that I never meant to hurt them. And though no one else understands what I have to do, maybe You will. If I *do* survive, then perhaps You'll allow me to accept that as a sign of Your divine approval. I don't want to go back, I want to *be* Stephanie, and if I can't do that, then I'd rather not live at all. But if You do allow me to come through, then I think I can promise that Stephanie will be a much nicer person than Keith ever was.'

KEITH

1
THE EARLY YEARS

My birth was an accident. Just how much of an accident no one fully appreciated until many years later. My father often used to say that I walked to the beat of a different drum – although I'm sure he had no idea of how prophetic his words would ultimately prove to be.

My father's family, the Hulls, originally came from Redhill in Surrey, where they owned a successful chain of fish and chip shops. Successful, that is, until one of their trusted managers absconded with the takings. After moving to Harpenden in Hertfordshire and finding himself unable to get planning permission to open a fish and chip shop there, my grandfather started a decorating business in which my father, Frederick, assisted whenever he was not working at his other job, on the railways. One of four children, my father later grew apart from his brothers and sister, so I have few recollections of my paternal aunts and uncles.

My mother, born Gladys Beryl Minall, came from far humbler origins. One of eight children, she lived in a small terraced cottage in an area known as The Folly on the outskirts of a picturesque Hertfordshire village called Wheathampstead. My mother's childhood was, by any standards, a hard one; on more than one occasion she and her brothers and sisters were placed in an orphanage when their parents were too ill to look after them. However, despite their poverty and the problems of having to sleep four to a bed in a tiny house with no running water, they remained a close-knit, loving family.

My parents married when they were both nineteen. Six months after the birth of my elder sister Pearl, Dad was struck down with a mysterious disease. My poor father had to endure over ten years of painful traction, repeated lumbar injections, numerous operations and, at one stage, the total encasement of his body in plaster for a period of three and a half years, before his doctors were able to diagnose the mysterious disease as ankylosing spondylitis and arrest it with a series of gold injections. Unfortunately, by the time he was finally allowed home to live with his family, all the main joints in his body had become rigid and he was virtually crippled for life.

At that time, social security and the welfare state were not yet in existence, so my mother was forced to experience again the poverty and deprivation of her childhood as she struggled to bring up my sister alone. In addition my father was unable to work on his return home, and dependent upon my mother to dress him and help perform all the personal tasks that the healthy take so much for granted. A variety of cleaning jobs enabled my mother to produce just enough to cover the rent and food and, though life must have been very difficult, Mum did what she has always done: she coped.

The one thing about my father's physical health that remained unimpaired was his virility. Within weeks of his release from hospital, an unforeseen and unwanted complication arose which forced him to ignore the doctor's pronouncements that he would never walk again, as well as their warnings that he was medically unfit to work, because my mother was pregnant with me. Obviously, Dad's disability made it extremely difficult for him to find work; even when he did, a succession of employers proved only too keen to exploit his situation by paying him very low wages. Undeterred, he developed a tenacity and strength of character that were to typify his lifelong fight against his disability – the same inherited qualities of courage that enabled me to make the greatest journey a human being can undertake.

My birth certificate still attests that Keith Michael Hull was born at the Oster Hill's Hospital for the Poor at St Albans, Hertfordshire on 25 May 1946. Although I was originally an unwanted child, when my parents took me home to 21 Weybourne close, Harpenden, where I was to spend my first eleven years, they were delighted that I was healthy, whole and very obviously male.

My father was a strict disciplinarian. A tall man, whose disability caused him to stoop and reduced his height to five feet nine, he propelled himself around with the help of two walking sticks, rarely allowing a smile or any warmth to lighten his countenance. This, coupled with thinning hair and spectacles which gave him the appearance of being older than he was (though, in fact, he still looks much the same today), gave an impression of a remarkably formidable and forbidding sort of character. I lived in fear of him until the day I got married. I don't know whether he was ever aware of how very much I longed for a display of love or even affection from him, and how disappointed and rejected I always felt at receiving none. To this day he remains a distant figure and I have never really been sure whether he is totally without emotion or, as I would rather believe, someone who considers showing emotion to be unmanly.

My mother, at five feet three, was fairly small, very slim and never still. Always concerned with helping others (who were usually in a better position than herself), she nevertheless has always been a strong, determined character who, once committed to a course of action, is completely unmovable.

Home was a typical 'two up, two down' terrace. The back door, which was reached through an alleyway separating the two middle houses, opened straight on to the living room, which contained my father's special chair sandwiched between a large valve radio on a shelf and the dining table. The floor was covered in linoleum which extended into the tiny kitchenette with its walk-in cold larder and old-fashioned gas stove. The stairs to the upper floor, which housed my parents' bedroom, the back bedroom – which I shared with Pearl for seven years until she left home – and a draughty, basic bathroom, could only be reached through the front room, which was reserved for high days and holidays. The entire house, apart from the living room, was always freezing cold because rationing was still in evidence and we couldn't get enough coal. Despite the fact that my father had found a job as a sheet metal worker, luxuries (those things that today we call necessities) were still conspicuous by their absence – fruit, in the shape of half a banana, was a weekly treat, while a bottle of Corona was a cause for celebration!

Pearl was undoubtedly favoured by my parents – particularly my father who, having missed the first ten years of her childhood, would often make a great fuss of her. But despite the fact that she was always being held up as a shining example, Pearl and I were very close until she left home. My father often berated me with comments like, 'Why can't you be more like your sister?' – though I don't suppose he ever dreamed I would take him quite so literally! Pearl was a paragon of perfect behaviour. One of life's naturally good people, she was appointed head girl at school and never did anything wrong. Unfortunately, by comparison I was considered the black sheep of the family. Certainly, my father would derisively condemn me as a cissy whenever I displayed cowardliness at the prospect of my weekly bath. It wasn't that I minded water, or even the bath itself. What filled me with dread were the terrifying antics of our ancient geyser, which was incapable of dispensing hot water without first undergoing a series of death-defying rituals before it would ignite. Its blood-curdling sound effects would have me petrified for hours afterwards.

Weekly baths aside, life up to the age of five was fairly uncomplicated. We kept in close contact with my mother's relatives and were frequent visitors at my Auntie Elsie and Uncle Ray's house. My mother's parents, who were extremely frail and hard of hearing, were looked after by my Auntie Kath and Uncle Reg, who lived with them at the same house that my mother had grown up in. My grandmother, a large lady with thinning hair, wore dentures, which she couldn't abide and would spit out at every opportunity, and a hearing aid which she took great delight in turning off whenever you spoke to her about her dentures. Because Auntie Elsie and Uncle Ray were both so involved building up their garage business their youngest daughter, my cousin Barbara, who was just a year younger than me, spent a great deal of time at our house, often staying with us for such long periods that we regarded each other as brother and sister rather than cousins. Young as I was then, I can still recall the Christmases we spent at Auntie Elsie's: the presents, the silver threepenny bits hidden in the Christmas pudding and, most memorable of all, settling down after lunch in front of that rarest of luxuries – a vintage TV set with a tiny, pink, nine-inch screen which was the envy of the entire neighbourhood.

Strangely enough, although I can't recollect the precise moment, it was around the age of five that I had my first conscious memory of the dream that was to haunt me continually. At first my recollections were minimal; I remembered only that in this dream I had been a girl. Later, I was to discover that in my dreams I was always a girl and only in my nightmares was I male.

I don't think anything can adequately prepare a small child for the trauma that is their first day at school. By the time that day came, I had already made up my mind that the prospect was not half so attractive to me as it obviously was to my parents and so, like many other children of five, I was a fairly reluctant recruit to the education system. With me perched on the back of my mother's bicycle, we laboriously climbed Pickford Hill, at the top of whose steep incline stood the imposing house of horror that was Batford Primary School. Too frightened to put on a brave face, I was discharged, crying, into the playground where, in common with my equally bewildered companions, I surveyed this vast, new, noisy, baffling world.

Like timid sheep we were herded together towards the cloak-room, where an intimidating teacher ordered us to select a hook upon which we were to hang our coats and satchels. The girls, on one side of the cloakroom, had hooks identified by a variety of teddies, dolls and fluffy, cutesy animals. Predictably, the boys' hooks had boats, trains and planes. Dutifully, I selected a train and claimed it with my coat. Just at that moment I noticed the approach of what was obviously from his demeanour the school bully in training. He was looking for a suitable target, and the inferior specimen he chose was me. Lunging for my coat, he threw it on the floor, replaced it with his own and then shoved me over. Stumbling, I fell backwards on to an object so painfully sharp that I immediately yelped, propelled myself forward and accidentally cannoned straight into my opponent. What happened next couldn't have been more bloody (or more fortuitous) had it been staged and rehearsed by a master stunt-arranger. Caught off balance by the impact, my hapless assailant tripped over his own satchel and fell heavily against the very peg he had fought for, gashing open his head so badly that he immediately collapsed at my feet in an unconscious bloody heap.

Chalk-white and still unconscious, the poor boy was carted off by ambulance to the local hospital. A peaceful week passed before he was well enough to return to class, by which time (and completely by chance), having gained the totally undeserved respect of my new school pals, I'd become a local hero and established a reputation that, while unfounded, was nevertheless to provide me with protection throughout the remainder of my six years at primary school.

Thus began eleven years of state education that were, supposedly, specifically designed to prepare this young lad for adulthood. Needless to say, though they weren't entirely wasted, they were hardly designed to prepare me for what life had in store.

Batford Primary School was a good two-mile walk from my home. Every day, summer and winter, no matter what the weather, my friends and I trudged unescorted to and from school. The shortest route took us down the steep slope of Crabtree Lane which, come winter and the much-prayed-for snow, was transformed into the perfect toboggan run. From there we would cross the ford of the River Lea at the bottom of the hill, skirt round by Batford Mill and then nip through the old deserted prisoner-of-war camp with its tall watchtower and rusty Nissen huts to emerge half a mile from Batford Primary.

With my new friends and our exciting adventures to look forward to on the way home, it didn't take me long to settle in. Towards the end of my first Christmas term I reached the highest pinnacle of primary school achievement: I was chosen to appear in the annual nativity play as one of the Three Wise Kings. Although fairly central to the storyline, my part, and the four words I had to memorize for it, hardly constituted adequate qualification for an Equity card in later life. Since our teacher was not one to give praise, I never knew whether my performance had come up to the exacting standards demanded of a troupe of five-year-olds – and much good would it have done me even if it had.

I had just passed my sixth birthday when I fell ill with yellow jaundice. It was an illness with unfortunate consequences at school. I felt decidedly queasy one morning and more than usually dreaded the school dinner. As I stared miserably at the lumpy mashed potatoes, pulverized meat and mushy, boiled vegetables adrift in a sea of watery gravy, I suddenly broke out in a sweat.

'Please, miss, may I be excused? I don't feel well,' I managed to squeak.

'Certainly not!' came the peremptory reply from the dinner supervisor. With a sadistic smile she advanced to my table and positioned herself menacingly beside me as I slowly forced the revolting mess down my throat and into my protesting stomach. No sooner was the last forkful in my mouth than the inevitable happened. I threw up with so much force that I managed to cover my plate, most of the table and everyone within three feet of me. Revenge was very sweet – my only regret was that I didn't feel well enough at the time to enjoy it.

Once diagnosed, I was ordered to stay off school for several weeks, which neatly enabled me to evade any form of retribution. Pearl caught the disease too and, unfortunately, suffered far worse than I did. However, once we were over the worst we were able to spend a great deal of time amusing each other. Eventually I recovered, and was sent back to school to enjoy my second Christmas there. And though none of us was aware of it then, that Christmas was also the last we were ever to celebrate together as a family.

The year 1953 was barely underway when a stranger by the

name of Douglas Joyce called at our house. That knock on the door – just one of the many doors Douglas Joyce risked having slammed in his face every day of his life – was to prove both unexpectedly fruitful for him and enormously influential in the shaping of my family's life. For Joyce was a Jehovah's Witness, and before too long he became a frequent and welcome visitor. My mother was the first to embrace the religion and, though my father was much slower to make the conversion (which meant he would have to forswear smoking), eventually he, too, became so staunch a member that he was ultimately elected to hold office. And, having become fired with religious fervour, my parents naturally observed all the rules. Thus Christmas, like so many other celebrations, became something that only other people's children were allowed to enjoy.

The common perception of a Jehovah's Witness is that of a religious fanatic who spends his or her life walking the streets in all weathers, knocking on doors at inconvenient times, and who would rather let a child die than allow a blood transfusion. But the truth is somewhat different.

Jehovah's Witnesses' central philosophy is that they should embrace the Bible wholly and literally – good and bad. It's by no means an easy religion, but I've always found them to be very sincere people who aren't in the least hypocritical. While many do undertake the biblical commandment that they should go out and preach to others, I think their courage, perseverance and continual good humour in the face of hostility, abuse or, at the very least, a series of closed doors, are much to be admired.

Interestingly enough, at precisely the same time as my parents became converted, our next door neighbour, a DIY freak who made our Sundays unbearable with his noisy banging and sawing from dawn to dusk, also found religion in the shape of the Plymouth Brethren. From that moment on he gave his Sundays to church, which earned my heartfelt approval as it meant that I could at last enjoy a peaceful – albeit very brief – lie-in before our newly acquired religious duties beckoned.

My parents' conversion had a dramatic effect on our lives. Suddenly there seemed to be endless meetings to attend. Tuesday evening, eight till nine, we had group Bible study at the home of a Witness called Vera Fawcett. I always enjoyed these meetings tremendously, not so much because of what I was learning but because the moment we finished studying Vera would ply me with food! Thursday evenings, too, were entirely taken up with meetings and eventually our whole family life began to revolve around our church, Bible study groups and fellow members.

Celebrations didn't just stop now we were converted – they went into reverse! The following Christmas was awful. In their attempt to ignore it, my parents went into overkill. There was no gaiety, no family get-together with Auntie Elsie, Uncle Ray and my cousins, no turkey, no Christmas pudding with silver three-penny bits hidden inside (in fact the food we ate that day was far inferior to what we would have had on any normal day) and, worst of all, no presents. And as if that wasn't bad enough, when I returned to school I found myself in the miserable position of being totally excluded from all the happy discussions about who had received what from Santa Claus – because, of course, I had nothing to contribute!

The changes, coming so abruptly and overwhelmingly, were very confusing and, as time passed, the rigid rules and disciplines of the faith forced me further and further apart from my friends and peers. In retrospect, it was the perfect preparation for a future in which I would be forced to stand apart from the crowd to a degree that few people experience. But even if I had known that then, I'm sure it would have brought little comfort.

Come rain, shine, snow and fog, I was made to tramp the streets beside my parents as they delighted in their new mission in life: the spreading of the word according to the gospel of the Jehovah's Witnesses. Every Sunday afternoon we would attend a public talk, which was often given by a visiting speaker from another congregation, and afterwards we would indulge in an hour-long study of the *Watchtower* magazine. Weekly reports had to be filed, stating how many hours we had spent knocking on doors. The more involved my mother became, the more often I would be dragged along to strangers' houses where my mother would lead study hour after study hour as she sought to convert – and save – as many souls as she could.

Every weekday morning I had to get up at seven to help Mum get Dad off to work, a journey he would make in an open-topped, open-sided invalid carriage. As our road was at the bottom of a hill, the only way to start this vehicle was for Mum and me to push it up to the top of the road and back down again with Dad inside. Once the motor was running, Dad would swing round at the bottom of the close and puff his way off to work followed by a plume of blue smoke. On one such occasion he overdid the turn at the bottom and, to our horror, his invalid carriage turned over. Panic ensued for several moments as we roused the neighbours to help right the vehicle. To our relief Dad was unhurt, but the accident had shaken him so much that after that he was always extremely careful when he swung the vehicle round at the bottom of the close. But that invalid carriage provided the few moments of closeness Dad and I were ever to enjoy together, when he'd allow me to ride in front of him and even, on occasions, let me take the steering wheel when the roads were quiet.

When I was seven, my parents bought me a bicycle. An ancient bone shaker, hand-painted in black, it was the most fearsome thing I'd ever laid eyes on. After Dad had left for work, Mum, determined that I would learn to ride it, would lift me, protesting, on to its uncomfortable saddle. Her method of instruction was basic, to say the least; as I wobbled from side to side in an effort to find my balance, she would alternately smack my legs and shout at me to pedal. Needless to say I proved an apt, though unwilling, pupil.

Pearl, who'd left school at fifteen and found a job at the same company where my father was employed, became more and more involved with the Witnesses, to the point where she even gave up one of her boyfriends because it was forbidden to marry outside the religion. When she was seventeen she decided to leave home and become a pioneer. Pioneers spend nearly all their time spreading the message by calling door to door. As the work is unpaid and often involves them being sent to live in another area, they have to rely on a part-time job to support themselves.

Life was totally dominated by the church, and gradually I found that the multitude of meetings were impinging on any time I might have available to play with my school friends. Naturally, this resulted in my becoming somewhat isolated and alienated from many of them, as my life was so different from theirs.

Dad's disabilities prevented him from fully exploiting his many abilities at work – though, to his credit, he did get promoted enough to control a large part of the production process. Obviously, his limitations caused him great frustration. But he was a determined man and he soon diverted his energies into his religion. I'm convinced that the very restrictions that prevented him from advancing his career were the fuel he burned in his fervent pursuit of progress within the organization of our religion. Respected for his leadership qualities and his total commitment, he soon became overseer of the Harpenden congregation. More of our Sundays were devoted to travelling further and further afield as he began to receive invitations to speak to other congregations.

By now, the dream that was to dominate my life had become an almost nightly occurrence. It invariably involved a girl at school who was a bit of a tomboy and her parents, who in the dream had always wanted a son instead of a daughter. For some strange reason this husband and wife kidnapped me, and then subjected me to an operation (the clinical details of which were never clear) which transformed me into their daughter and their daughter into the son they had always wanted. Although the dream might vary from time to time, the basic details always remained the same: I was always transformed into a girl.

When my cousin Barbara started staying with us for increasingly longer periods, my life became a little bit more normal in that I was allowed more free time to play with her. In fact, it was with Barbara's help that I discovered the essential physical differences between the sexes. Nothing untoward happened, I hasten to add. We merely did what most young children do: we indulged in a practical demonstration and close inspection of what is commonly termed '*la différence*'.

Barbara and I became very friendly with two children by the name of Susan Lawrence and Rodney Seabrook, and we spent many happy hours in Rodney's garage dressing up in a variety of costumes and performing plays for our own amusement. After some months, we thought we had developed Snow White and the Seven Dwarfs into what we considered to be a fairly professional presentation (despite the fact that we lacked the necessary numbers to cover all the parts) and, emboldened by self-praise, we marched down to the public hall, demanded to see the organizer and asked to book the hall for a series of theatrical performances. To his credit, this gentleman neither laughed at us, nor told us off for wasting his time. Instead he merely informed us solemnly, and seemingly regretfully, that, alas, the hall was already fully booked for the next two years.

Thwarted in our thespian ambitions, we nevertheless continued to employ Rodney's garage as our own private theatre. Although we all enjoyed ourselves tremendously, I probably gained far more from those innocent dressing-up sessions than the others; for they were my first experience of wearing girls' clothes.

Despite the fact that my strange dreams were both frightening and confusing, there was something about dressing as a girl that gave me a strange sense of contentment. Somehow it seemed to feel 'right'. The moment I put a dress on I felt less clumsy, more natural and more peaceful than I ever remembered feeling before. With hindsight, I now can identify a number of clues that pointed to a potential problem, but at the time, though I intuitively knew I was 'different', it never occurred to me to look for any profound meaning. Although my dreams were becoming disturbing enough for me to dread going to sleep at night, I still managed to dismiss them from my mind in the morning and concentrate only on the pleasures – or the duties – of the day that lay ahead.

At first I badly missed being able to play with Barbara, Susan and Rodney on Sundays once that day became exclusively devoted to the Sect. But in time I grew used to the constant meetings and even to the way in which our religion encroached on every aspect of our life. I'm sure that, as far as my parents were concerned, religion was (and still is) their life. And even the drama of two particular events that stand out in my memory weren't enough to interfere with their devotion to their religious duties.

The first drama was caused by my father's newly found interest in brewing. Someone had given Dad a recipe for brewing ginger beer, a fairly harmless substance, he believed. Having assembled a collection of old Corona bottles with china stoppers held securely in place by metal wires, Dad applied himself to his new hobby with almost the same fervour he applied to the Sect. On this particular Sunday Dad and I were patiently waiting, immaculate in our Sunday best, for Mum to come downstairs. 'Come on, son, we've just got time to nip down to the shed to see how the beer's coming along,' Dad said.

Once there, he inspected the bottles. However, as that didn't reveal much, he then picked one up and started to ease the metal wire back to release the stopper. Suddenly, there was an explosive noise and a great fountain of gaseous, still fermenting ginger beer shot straight out of the bottle with all the force of a rocket ship leaving earth. Unlike a rocket ship, though, it met an impediment – our ancient, rusty, corrugated-iron shed roof! With nowhere else to go, the sticky beer, by now combined with years of rust, rained down on us in an avalanche of indelibly staining, muddy liquid. We looked such a fright when we emerged from the shed that my mother didn't know whether to laugh or cry. Instead, she shooed us inside the house, stripped our clothes off, scrubbed us until we shone and lectured us both all the way to the meeting house. The rare experience of finding myself accompanied in the doghouse by no less a person than my own father made me feel closer to him in those moments than I'd ever felt before!

The second dramatic event occurred when, once again dressed up in my 'going to meeting' best, I was riding my bike up and down the close while waiting for my parents to come out. Suddenly I caught sight of Barry, the fourteen-year-old son of another neighbour, messing around with an old motorbike on the other side of our road. Intrigued by the noise and the smoke, I propped my bike against a garden wall and joined a group of other local children who were lounging against the wall avidly watching Barry's antics.

Keenly aware that we were giving him all our admiring attention, Barry started showing off by mounting the bike and kick-starting it with a display of cool nonchalance designed to show us he was an experienced rider. To his horror – and our pop-eyed, cruel delight – the powerful machine roared into life, jerked off its stand and shot across the road towards us at lightning speed. By now totally out of control, the motorbike crashed straight into my bike. The problem was that, though the motorbike stopped, Barry didn't. Still in mid-flight, and with me right bang in the middle of his flight path, Barry collided into me with such force that we both soared over the wall and crash-landed in a heap in the flower bed on the other side. Thirty seconds earlier, or two feet to the right, and my life – and my problems – would have ceased to be. As it was, although I was badly bruised and grazed, no great damage had been done to me. My parents, always anxious to avoid a fuss, promised Barry's parents that in return for the repair or replacement of my mangled bike they wouldn't take the matter any further. Which was pretty fair of them considering that, as Barry was under age, uninsured, untaxed and had committed half the motoring offences in the book, the police would have treated the matter far more seriously.

As vivid as that memory of Barry is, it was his younger sister, Lucy, who was to provide me with far more reason to remember the family. For it was Lucy who was to play such a significant role in the furtherance of my sex education a few years later.

Not that it was being totally neglected in the meantime for, as time went on, the lofty thespian ideals of my little group of friends rapidly began to degenerate into more fundamental pursuits as sexual awareness began to dawn. On one particularly hot summer day, the four of us decided to cool off in the paddling pool at Batford Park. Still wearing our swimming costumes, we then wandered up to a bushy, overgrown stretch of land that had once been used as a football field, to the side of which was an enormous cornfield. Bored and listless, we half-heartedly played a few games for a while before Susan decided to liven up the proceedings by daring Rodney to remove his trunks. The moment he'd obliged, she grabbed the shorts and raced off into the cornfield, whooping and waving them above her head like a prized trophy. Poor Rodney, wearing nothing but a stricken look, followed in hot pursuit – watched, in utter amazement, by an elderly couple who were out walking their dog.

That day marked a turning point, and from then on the guilt we all began to feel about our relatively innocent dressing up games in Rodney's garage caused us first to become more furtive about what we were doing, and then to abandon our games altogether. After that, my education into the mysteries of the opposite sex began in earnest.

I'd developed a passion for cinematography after being given a second-hand film projector. My collection was sparse, to say the least, but that didn't deter me from roping in Murray and Paul Gray, two younger lads who lived next door with their mother (their father having moved out some time before), as my captive audience at repeated screenings of the only three 8 mm films I possessed. On one occasion, desperate to improve my cinematic presentation techniques, I waited until my mother had left for yet another Bible reading class at the home of one of her latest converts, then popped next door to persuade Murray and Paul to come back with me and sit through another interminable session of Mickey Mouse and Popeye.

'Hello, Keith,' said Mrs Gray as she opened the front door. 'If you've come round for Murray and Paul, I'm afraid you've missed them. They went out to play some time ago,' she explained. 'Still, never mind, you can come in for a few minutes and give me a hand.'

Now Mrs Gray was far from being an attractive woman, but she did have one remarkable asset that caused much comment amongst the pre-pubertal lads around our way. She possessed the most remarkable bosom any of us had ever seen and, though we were still a bit young to waste much thought on bosoms in general, Mrs Gray's monumental attributes had often been the subject of innocent speculation as we'd pondered the feat of engineering that kept them aloft.

Alone in the house, with a kettle full of steaming water cooling rapidly in the sink, my interruption must have given Mrs Gray a bright idea, for no sooner had I followed her into the kitchenette than she began to strip off her clothes (the amazing feat of engineering and all) and invited me to help wash the very bosom that had held us all enthralled. And that was the moment I first discovered a flaw in my parents' strict code of behavioural conduct – having been brought up to be polite, obedient and helpful at all times, I didn't know how to say no.

What took place over the next two years between Mrs Gray and the naïve and nervous – but always polite – boy I was then, would, I imagine, be termed child abuse today. Whether I derived any satisfaction or even pleasure from those encounters I honestly cannot recall. And although Mrs Gray never made any attempt to coerce me into actual intercourse (given my youth, I suspect it would have been mission impossible anyway), she always seemed to stage-manage a scenario in which I was engaged in washing or massaging specific little (and very often large) parts of her anatomy while she, in return, concentrated her attention on even smaller parts of me.

Despite the fact that I instinctively knew my parents would not approve of these encounters (and I, myself, regarded them with a certain amount of guilt and fear), I didn't do anything to prevent them because, while I knew it was wrong, Mrs Gray was providing me with all the unaccustomed, warmth and affection I so desperately craved. Perhaps that's why I plucked up the courage to tell her of my experiences dressing up in girls' clothes. Far from being shocked, as I had feared, she immediately went out and bought me an entire outfit of suitably sized girls' clothing; and from that moment on, whenever we were alone together at her house I dressed as a girl.

This spurred me on to collect my own motley assortment of mismatched skirts, blouses and dresses, most of which I scavenged from sites where gypsies had recently encamped. Whenever the opportunity arose, I'd make for some isolated spot where, for a few brief hours, I'd be content to sit and read or think, enjoying a peace and tranquillity that had eluded me for most of my life.

Outside of this glimpse into a feminine world, life continued much the same as before. The constant meetings, preachings, studying and work of the Jehovah's Witnesses dominated our entire life. But on the rare evenings when I was allowed out to play, I'd join the other children playing in the street and we'd make nuisances of ourselves as we played the kind of games that all children love and all adults hate. Knock Down Ginger was a great favourite of ours. This entailed tying cotton to our neighbours' door knockers, hiding behind a convenient bush or garden wall and then repeatedly tugging on the cotton until our hapless victims became irate at continually opening their front doors only to find nobody there.

Another of our favourite pastimes was lighting camp fires on the overgrown football pitch. One day in the summer holidays Rodney and I built a huge camp fire that we were very proud of – we kept dashing off to forage more fuel to keep it burning. However, when we returned from one such foray we were aghast to find that the fire had spread to the surrounding dry grass and, despite all our frantic attempts to stamp it out, showed every sign of turning into a blazing inferno. Not wanting to be connected with the disaster, Rodney and I beat a hasty retreat to our respective garden sheds where we hid in mounting terror as the clanging of the fire engine bells grew louder and louder. Fortunately, the fire brigade doused the flames before they had a chance to engulf the entire town. Unfortunately I once again had to face the wrath of my father, who by now was totally convinced that everything I did was at worst a mortal sin, at best destined to end in disaster.

All too soon, my life began to change. With secondary school looming large, we moved to a new three-bedroomed semi-bungalow my parents had had built just a few hundred yards away in Crabtree Lane, on the very same waste ground site where Barbara, Susan, Rodney and I had had such fun. Having scrimped and scraped to afford the house, by the time we moved in we were flat broke. Still, at least we could look forward to a winter of relative luxury with part central heating and, best of all as far as I was concerned, there would be no noisy, frightening geyser to contend with at bathtime!

Life had taken a turn for the better and, even though I still came out in a cold sweat every time I crawled between the bedsheets at night, fearing what my strange dreams might reveal, I looked forward to joining the 'big boys and girls' at Manland Secondary School. It never occurred to me that becoming one of the 'big boys' would mean having to contend with the horrors of puberty and the flattering (though privately puzzling) interest of girls – an interest that was to lead me into a variety of bizarre sexual encounters that were destined to con-firm that, as far as the female sex was concerned, I seemed to be totally lacking in everything it took to be a man. And, as I never had any inclinations towards my own sex either, where did that leave me? My future, and the awful truth which would take years for me to acknowledge, were about to start closing in.

2
BECOMING A MAN

Although I was looking forward to starting secondary school, when the day finally dawned I found myself filled with an apprehension that was only mitigated by the fact that my pal Rodney was moving up with me. To my consternation I found that we were expected to take our sporting activities very seriously indeed. Never having been particularly athletic, the moment I set eyes on our games master, a brawny specimen bristling with machismo, I knew I was going to be in for a bad time. I dreaded changing in front of the other boys and loathed having to use the communal showers, convinced that without the protection of my clothes all the other lads would immediately see that I was 'different' and, as schoolboys are wont to do, make my life a misery.

Cricket practice was sheer torture as, determined to 'make a man' of me, the games master would insist on sending me in to bat. I'd stand there with my bat bravely poised, right until the moment I saw that rock-hard ball leave the bowler's hand and come hurtling towards me. Then I'd go into retreat with a quick backwards shuffle that would place at least three feet between me, the wicket and the massacre I was convinced would be my fate were I to remain at my post.

But the horrors of cricket were as nothing compared to the legalized blood sport they called soccer. How anyone could actually enjoy the prospect of spending ninety minutes on a football pitch with twenty-two rampaging boys and forty-four thundering legs intent on kicking hell out of each other has always been beyond me. Fortunately, my classmates were as anxious to avoid having me on their side as I was to join them, so a compromise was struck: I would assume the role of referee. The problem was I knew absolutely nothing about the rules of football – consequently, every time a player was about to score I'd intervene with a sharp blast on my whistle as if he were off-side. With each successive game my unpopularity grew.

Given my obvious dislike of all sports, the games master was perplexed at my apparent enthusiasm for cross-country running. Then he discovered that, after leading the field for the first half mile or so, I'd surreptitiously drop out of the race and make straight for Auntie Elsie's house where I'd be plied with drinks, cakes and sweets before coolly rejoining my sweating classmates on the last half-mile of their return journey.

When I was made a prefect in my fourth year, no one was more surprised than my parents and no one was more disgusted than the games master! But even that accolade was earned more by default than merit, and it was my sister Pearl who was the unwitting cause: apparently the head teacher, Mr Bloxham, found it impossible to believe that any brother of Pearl's could be *all* bad!

My first (and last) ambitious project in woodwork class was a tea trolley which took most of my five years at secondary school to complete and provided a perfect weekly excuse for 'money for materials' – half of which went to support my newly acquired 'habit' – illicit smoking. When my parents enrolled me in private music and singing classes with a lady called Miss Toyer, it didn't take me long to discover a better use for my time and their money. Inevitably, after several weeks' non-attendance I got caught out and the tea trolley, which had been progressing at a cracking pace while I had an alternative source of cigarette funds, once more slowed down in production.

Our favourite haunt at that time was Le Capri café in Harpenden village. It was run by a chap called Benny who, no matter how much time (or how little money) we spent hanging around sipping espresso coffee and smoking umpteen cigarettes, remained unfailingly cheerful and chatty. My one and only period of truancy from school, which lasted a whole week, was spent almost entirely at Le Capri with Rodney and a few of the lads, plotting exciting (and foolhardy) escapades. It was there that we first dreamed up the idea of sneaking out of our houses in the middle of the night. As I lived in a bungalow this proved to be remarkably easy, though how the others managed to climb out of a second-storey window and shin down a drainpipe without being caught, I'll never know. On one of these midnight excursions we decided to paint a slogan on the side of a big railway bridge that spanned the main A6 road. For years afterwards, whenever I drove down that road and saw the words "KEEP BRITAIN GREAT" in enormous capital letters on the side of the bridge, I would feel faint, wondering how I had managed to conquer my fear of heights to take part in such a dangerous prank.

Not long afterwards, the husband of a Bible study acquaintance of my mother's went to Spain, leaving his large motorbike safely (or so he thought) in storage at our house. The temptation proved too great, and before long Rodney and I had developed the knack of quietly wheeling the bike out of the garage at night and rolling it down to the bottom of the hill where, safely out of earshot, we'd kick-start it into life and embark on a hair-raising, heart-stopping ride at great speed around the Hertfordshire countryside. It makes me shudder now when I think of two fourteen-year-old boys with no insurance, no road tax, no crash helmets and no protective clothing doing seventy miles per hour down those dark, unlit country roads when our parents thought we were safely tucked up in bed.

Predictably, we got caught – not by the police, but by someone whose wrath was far more terrifying: my mother. We had sneaked the bike back into the garage, bidden each other a whispered goodnight and then, just as I had one leg over the sill of my bedroom window, the light snapped on. I froze in horror at the sight of my mother framed in the doorway with a grim expression on her face. Convinced they had given birth to the biggest sinner of all time, my parents refused to believe that my adolescent pranks were fairly normal for a boy of my age – if I'd been sneaking out at night, then it *had* to be for some deeply illegal or immoral purpose. It must have been months before they were able to get a good night's sleep again.

So my nocturnal wanderings came to an abrupt halt. Not so my smoking, however. Despite all my efforts to keep my sinful 'habit' concealed, I regularly got caught. If I'd been to the cinema, I'd rub my fingers on the brickwork outside the house to remove all trace of nicotine stains and stuff myself with extra strong mints to mask the smell. But as my mother had the nose of a bloodhound all my efforts were in vain, and time and time again I'd be on the receiving end of lectures about my evil ways as yet another lighter and pack of cigarettes were confiscated.

Outwardly, I appeared to be no different from any other boy of my age. Inwardly, however, I was becoming more and more confused. My friends were clearly acquiring a sexual interest in girls, and they'd talk about it a great deal. It seemed strange to me that I didn't share their enthusiasm, but again I didn't dare tell anyone how I felt – it was too private, too confusing and far too difficult for *me* to explain or deal with – let alone anyone else. Besides, I was sure everyone would think I was gay; after all, people are expected to be one way or the other, and if a boy's not attracted to girls there's only one other conclusion that people normally reach. But in my case they would have been wrong. Although I was a very sensitive boy who would often be moved to tears in private by sad songs, books and films, I definitely wasn't attracted to boys either.

For any normal boy, being brought up a Jehovah's Witness would have been a heaven-sent opportunity as the girls of our faith were banned from dating anyone outside the religion. But for me it proved only to be a source for yet more embarrassing and confusing episodes – particularly as I was the only teenage male in our congregation. I had one or two innocent relationships with girls which involved a lot of hand-holding and a little kissing, which I didn't mind in the least, but when I met Sandra I soon realized I was totally out of my depth.

Sandra was a well-built girl who lived nearby and went to the same school as me. I enjoyed her company and was quite happy to go out with her, to hold her hand and even, when I couldn't avoid it, kiss her. But, as I very soon discovered, that was tame stuff to Sandra, who was not only sexually experienced but had every intention of continuing her education with me. I tried everything I could to prolong the kissing and hand-holding stage, but it soon became clear that what Sandra wanted was sex – not a romantic little seduction, but hot, passionate sex, right then and there, and with someone whom for some strange reason she was convinced knew how to do it!

With mounting fear and apprehension I panicked as she insisted on dictating the pace. My first mistake was to display my inexperience when I fumbled with the hooks of her bra, which only caused her to push me impatiently away and undo it herself. My second mistake was in pretending to be so overwhelmed by her charms that I spent far too long exploring her breasts with my hands and mouth – silently hoping and praying that things would stop there. Inside my head a million questions were vying for answers. Should I run? What would she do or say if I did? Should I give her what she obviously wanted? How could I when, physically, I was totally unmoved? Should I refuse her? What would she say if I did? After all, it's usually the girl who refuses the boy, not the other way round!

Impatient with my ditherings, Sandra discarded her knickers. And then I knew I was *really* in trouble. What I needed now was either a step-by-step instruction manual or a quick run through an educational film. I'd heard stories in the playground, but I wasn't sure how accurate or reliable they were. I knew the vernacular for the hidden parts of male and female bodies, but no one had even hinted at the existence of such a thing as a clitoris – and if they had, in my ignorance I would probably have thought it was a plant.

Still fumbling around, I was beginning to find the whole exercise a bit messy and smelly – but worse was to come. Determined to accomplish the deed, Sandra speedily yanked off my clothes in search of a prey which she probably imagined to be a throbbing, thrusting monster just waiting to be let loose, but in reality was still a relaxed, curled-up little worm! I reckoned without Sandra's determination. If she was disappointed she hid it well as she commenced a series of moves designed to excite me. But eventually even she had to concede defeat.

We dressed in stony silence. Walking home, she brushed off my attempts to hold her hand, and when we reached her house she abruptly walked 'through the gate without so much as a goodbye. From that day on she never spoke to me again. I was mortified and humiliated, particularly when I saw her giggling behind her hands with her girlfriends and pointing derisively in my direction.

Shortly afterwards she started going out with Richard Church, who had a reputation as the class stud; predictably, before long the story of my dismal failure spread through the school. I was ridiculed to the point where my life became so unbearable I decided it was time to become 'ill'. This was accomplished by the simple expedient of cutting my toe, smearing blood all over a handkerchief and pretending to my horrified mother that the blood had been coughed up. I'm sure the doctor didn't believe one word of my story. Nevertheless I was given two weeks off school, and as I hid from the shame of my disastrous experience I prayed every day that my schoolmates would have forgotten the incident by the time I returned.

Each night I still dreamed about being kidnapped and forced to undergo an operation to transform me into a girl. For many years this dream centred on a girl in my class called Penelope Gould who, while she wasn't especially pretty, did have an exquisite figure. I used to spend hours gazing at her, lost in a dream of changing places with her and imagining what it would be like to be her, but still I couldn't bring myself to discuss this dream with anyone. Although I knew absolutely nothing about transsexuals, something inside me told me that my dreams, my lack of sexual interest in girls and my secret desire to dress in female clothing would probably be considered abnormal – and I had no desire to risk any more scorn than I had already experienced.

After the Sandra episode I decided it would be far safer to stick with girls who were Jehovah's Witnesses, reasoning that, as all forms of sexual contact between unmarried people were banned, I would always have a 'get out' clause. It didn't occur to me until much later that a girl's religious beliefs didn't necessarily counteract the effects of nature and her libido!

My next relationship lasted several months. Sylvia Monkton, who later married the brother of Hank Marvin of the Shadows, was a nice girl in every sense of the word. Our relationship, which was strictly confined to the innocent pleasures of kissing and hand-holding, provided me with the kind of healing therapy I so badly needed at that time.

After Sylvia I started seeing a fellow Witness, Vivienne, who, though never truly a girlfriend, did play a significant part in trying to sort out my 'problem'. Vivienne pursued me quite relentlessly and, fearing a repeat of the earlier humiliating episode with Sandra, I made a brave decision to inform Vivienne of my difficulties before events reached a critical stage, in the hope that this would ward off any passes. Once again, my naïvety failed to take into account that there's nothing a woman likes so much as a challenge! Totally forgetting all about her own sexual satisfaction, Vivienne reasoned that there must be *something* that would turn me on – all we had to do was try everything in the book until we found a solution. Her lack of selfishness and her commitment to her 'project' proved remarkable, and over the next few months we progressed through scenarios that ranged from her dressing up in stockings, suspenders and every conceivable 'sexy' outfit known to man, via dirty language and bondage to mild spanking. Vivienne's attitude was like that of a detached clinician who is quietly determined to succeed, while mine was one of resignation. I didn't particularly like the games we were playing, but I didn't know how to stop them.

That may sound like a pathetic excuse, but it's important to bear in mind the enormous peer pressure on the young to conform. As a boy I was expected to have girlfriends, expected to have sexual experiences and expected to be normal in every way, and as I so desperately wanted to be normal – or at the very least to *appear* to be normal – it was easier to go along with events than to resist and run the risk of yet more humiliation.

Besides, there was always the chance that Vivienne might just be able to 'cure' me. But that wasn't to be, for soon afterwards she became pregnant by somebody else and was despatched by her parents to a home for wayward girls. I received several friendly letters from her while she was in the home, and one of them inevitably fell into my mother's hands. This provided conclusive proof in my parents' minds that I was a lost cause, and conclusive proof in my own mind that there was something seriously wrong with me.

One might think that after such episodes I would have steered clear of the opposite sex; but I honestly enjoyed the company of girls and, provided things didn't get out of hand, I was still quite happy to have girlfriends – particularly as, for some strange reason, girls seemed to find *me* so attractive. Although I wasn't aware of it at the time, in retrospect I can see that my submissiveness with women must have been partly due to the incident with Sandra. I was particularly anxious to avoid any situation which might call attention to my 'difference', and having so many girls chasing me helped provide the perfect cover. So many incidents with so many girls somehow or other came to light that everyone was convinced I had a Casanova complex. I'm sure my parents thought I was a sex maniac in the making, and the lads I knew were certain I was having the time of my life, which was really quite ironic. However, thanks to the next girl I met I was able to sustain the notion that I was a full-blooded, healthy male, and so nobody was any the wiser.

Although I can't recall her name, the incident itself was so terrifying that I've never been able to forget it. I met the girl when her family joined our congregation. We became good friends, and one Sunday night after the meeting she came home with me to drink coffee and play records as my parents were going to be away for the night. I had no ulterior motive, but she obviously did because before too long we were frolicking on the floor completely naked. I remember she had a superb figure with very large breasts, and all I kept thinking was, ' My God, I wish I had a figure like that!'

Unbeknown to me, my parents had asked Ray Taylor, our congregation overseer, to keep an eye on me while they were away. Having stupidly neglected to lock the back door, I was to be humiliated once again – it's extremely difficult to remain dignified when someone walks in unannounced, switches on the light and finds you absolutely stark naked with a girl! Mr Taylor was so shocked that all he could do was order me to get dressed, take the girl home and come straight back. Quaking with terror and a sense of impending doom, I set off with her to walk the two miles or so to her house.

The girl was clearly far less distressed than I was, because as we passed the common she dragged me into the bushes and, despite all my protests, insisted we finish what she had started earlier. Convinced I would never get out of there until I complied, I decided the best thing to do was find some other way of giving her the satisfaction she so desperately sought. And that's when I made the discovery that to give is far more rewarding than to receive – for some women, oral sex is not only a perfect substitute for the real thing, it can also earn a guy a lot of brownie points as a caring, unselfish lover. But needless to say, when my parents learned what Ray Taylor had discovered, they were horrified and more furious than I'd ever seen them.

By now I'd reached the obvious conclusion that I just wasn't physically equipped for sex. So when I met Margaret Oakley, who at fifteen was a year younger than me, sweetly innocent and painfully shy, I was enormously relieved – particularly when I found that nothing more was expected of me than chaste kisses and long, hand-in-hand walks. Margaret and I spent a great deal of time together over the next two years, though rarely alone as we'd either be in the company of our parents at one of our houses or surrounded by fellow members of our congregation at meetings. Perhaps it was our shared innocence that made me feel Margaret was particularly special; certainly, she was the first girl that I ever *really* cared for.

My parents still insisted I attend all the meetings of our congregation, and these, together with my friendship with Margaret and my work for O-levels, left very little time for anything else. Mum and Dad were totally against my staying on at school. They believed that, as Armageddon was imminent, further education was a complete waste of time. Though Armageddon never came, they stuck solidly to this attitude throughout; later on, whenever I told them of my career successes, they would quote such biblical sayings as 'It's better to store up treasures in heaven than on earth' and 'it's harder for a rich man to enter the kingdom of heaven than for a camel to get through the eye of a needle', so I needed every bit of self-motivation that I could muster.

During my last year at school I worked at Uncle Ray and Auntie Elsie's garage in the evenings, serving petrol; as it was right next door to the local cinema I was able to provide myself with a constant supply of cigarettes and chocolates. My job also provided a handy excuse for not attending evening meetings. Unfortunately, that meant I didn't have much time to see Margaret either, so gradually our relationship began to dwindle. When I saw her one evening walking along the road hand-in-hand with another boy, I knew it was over altogether. I felt devastated and cried copious tears over what I considered to be the ultimate betrayal, but as time passed I eventually came to terms with my loss.

Even after exams were over we were still required to attend school until the end of term; the only exception was for job interviews. Rodney and I must have applied for every job that was advertised, just so that we could skive off school for a day. Rodney answered an ad for a lab research assistant at Adhesive Tapes Ltd, famous for Sellotape. Pretending to have an interview too, I accompanied him on the day trip to Boreham Wood. Immediately after Rodney's interview I was called in and, though I protested that I had not sent in an application and was merely along for the ride, the manager not only insisted on interviewing me but at the end offered me a job at the princely sum of £5 a week.

And so it was that I left school with four O-levels and a grand total of twenty other useless qualifications that are no longer recognized. In common with many youngsters, I'd reached the end of my schooling with no clear idea of what I wanted to do. And as I didn't seem to possess any great skills for the commercial world, my £5-a-week job seemed as good a place as any to start, despite having to travel over twenty miles to get there.

Life at Sellotape was fun. All the lab assistants were young, we all got on well together and practical jokes were frequently played to relieve the boredom and monotony of the job itself. One of our favourite tricks was to smear the black, sticky mixture which was used to form the base of insulation tape all over the earpiece of a black telephone receiver. We'd then go through to another lab, partitioned off by a glass room divider, and ring the extension. The unfortunate person who took the call invariably ended up with a messy ear that took hours of scrubbing to restore to its former state.

Another favourite involved the use of acetone which, when sprayed, evaporates into an invisible cloud of cold vapour. In the summer we'd climb up on to the flat roof of the building where, with the aid of a giant laboratory syringe, we'd spray the acetone over the side. As acetone is heavier than air it naturally descended to engulf anyone who might be enjoying the hot weather below, and within seconds would transform them into a startled, shivering wreck. On one occasion when some of the staff were horsing around we unwittingly discovered another, far more interesting, result when one of the lab staff squirted acetone down the lab coat of an attractive female research assistant. Acetone has a dissolving action upon nylon, and we had accidentally stumbled on the quickest method of denuding a woman yet devised by man!

As part of my training I attended Welwyn College, where I studied physics and chemistry as a day release student. As both the college and the factory were quite some distance from home I'd bought myself first a 70cc Capri scooter to make the journey more convenient, and then, when that gave out on me, a second-hand 125cc Lambretta. This vehicle served me admirably throughout the spring and summer months, but winter snow and ice made the journey far more hazardous. One day while travelling to work the roads were so treacherous that, when I attempted to brake as a bus cut across my path, I skidded straight into it, flew over the top and landed neatly on the platform. Fortunately I was unhurt, but my pride suffered a devastating blow in the face of the conductor's and passengers' obvious hilarity. Strangely enough, problems with my various modes of transport always seemed to bring out the best in my father, who never minded how much time he spent tinkering around with them. Sadly, though, they were the only occasions when I felt even remotely close to him.

I was still working at the garage in the evenings, and my frequent visits to the cinema foyer to stock up on cigarettes and sweets paid off when one of the staff informed me they had a vacancy for a part-time projectionist. Given my interest in cinematography, I jumped at the chance. The owner of the cinema was a grand old lady called Mrs Dempsey. The staff consisted of two managers, a cashier, a girl who worked in the kiosk selling sweets, drinks and cigarettes, a cleaner, a senior projectionist and two usherettes – Paula and Veronica, who were sisters.

Projection boxes in those days differed greatly from the modern, highly technological affairs of today. Each complete film took up several reels, which required changing every twenty minutes or so. The approaching changeover was signalled by a little white circle that would flash up on the top right-hand corner of the screen to warn the projectionist that it was time to start the motor to enable the next projector to gather sufficient speed, followed by another circle which indicated that it was time to switch the picture and sound from one projector to the next. The changeover was always timed to coincide with a change in scene, and if the switch was carried out by an expert it was virtually undetectable to the audience. Finished reels then had to be rewound and placed safely back in the can for the next showing. Obviously it was extremely important to be highly organized and efficient, as failure to rewind or keep the cans of film stacked in the right order could lead to disaster.

The projected light source was generated by burning carbon rods, with the necessary gap between the rods being controlled by a slow-moving, motor-driven track. This was subject to all kinds of problems as the rods tended to burn at different speeds, which meant they required frequent manual adjustments, and during a lightning storm they would invariably flicker out.

The projection box itself was completely soundproof, and there was an internal speaker with which we could communicate with the audience should the need arise. We also had our own secret alarm system in case of emergencies: fading in 'Land of Hope and Glory' over the soundtrack signalled a major emergency such as a fire, which required the complete evacuation of the cinema. The procedure was that the usherettes would throw open the emergency exits while the cashier would grab the takings box and run for her life to the garage next door. But these carefully rehearsed plans all went wrong one night just as we had begun to run through a new programme. Unbeknown to any of us, 'Land of Hope and Glory' featured as part of the film's soundtrack. This of course precipitated our emergency evacuation procedure, which all went very smoothly indeed. Unfortunately, as we'd had our speaker turned off in the box the senior projectionist and I were totally unaware that after that point we were playing to an empty auditorium!

Shortly after that event the senior projectionist fell out with the manager and handed in his notice; his job was offered to me. Fired with a sense of increased responsibility, omnipotence and an extra few shillings a week, I puffed up with pride and assumed complete control.

We were required by law to provide a secondary lighting system in case of a power cut, so that the Exit signs would always remain lit and enable the audience to escape safely during any emergency. The chloride batteries we used were frequently failing and the manager, who had been trying to work out a useful alternative, suggested placing night lights behind the Exit signs. Theoretically it was a good idea; practically it proved to be disastrous.

I arrived one evening to find that the chloride batteries had suffered a total breakdown during the afternoon matinee. The night lights were duly lit, and we had just begun the evening performance when the phone rang in the projection box. A panic-stricken usherette announced that there was a fire in the auditorium and begged me to rush down with a step-ladder and a fire extinguisher.

It quickly became clear that the flimsy Exit signs, which were made of cut-out wood heavily gilded with a highly flammable material, had caught light. Quick as a flash I pointed the nozzle of the extinguisher at the signs and sprayed them liberally. Unfortunately the main lighting bulbs inside, which had become overheated from the flames, reacted to the cold dousing by exploding, and showering very fine shards of glass all over the place. To make matters worse, other Exit signs around the auditorium caught light at the same time as the spool of film ran out, which meant that all that hit the screen was a blinding white light. Some of the audience had lingered behind to watch the fun as the cinema staff ran around in blind panic, squirting extinguishers wherever flames appeared and then ducking and diving to avoid the flying sparks as the bulbs exploded. It was like Bonfire Night and the Fourth of July all rolled into one, and though we eventually got the situation under control I'm convinced that most of our audience went home that night with far more vivid memories of the free entertainment the cinema staff provided than of the comedy film they had paid to see!

Although I tried hard to be diligent, efficient and professional, being the only person in the projection box meant that with a full three-hour programme of cartoons, advertising and two feature films, lights to control, records to put on for the intervals, curtains to open and close and umpteen reel changes in between, I was on the go for the entire evening. And although I was a reasonably good projectionist, inevitably there were times when I either forgot to rewind a film or showed the reels in the wrong sequence. Whenever these disasters occurred, I often wondered how many cinemagoers went home totally perplexed by the plot or convinced that they'd wasted their money on a rotten film, when in fact I had simply missed out one of the reels and cut a full twenty minutes of the action! Eventually I had to leave the cinema – not because I was bored or particularly wanted to leave, but because the antics of Paula and Veronica, the two usherettes, were getting beyond my control.

Paula, the plumper, older sister, had taken to visiting me in the projection box, locking the door behind her and subjecting me to a revolting rendition of the dance of the seven veils which had been performed centuries before – and far more successfully – by Salome. Paula was not what you would call a subtle girl, and when it came to blatant sexuality she knew no equal. In fact, so bold did she become that I lived in nightly terror of being caught in a compromising position or, worse, having to go home with ripped underwear or lipstick on my clothing.

The more I resisted her advances, the more determined she became. After several unsuccessful weeks of what I'm sure she felt was irresistible behaviour she enlisted the help of her sister, Veronica. Together they tricked me into turning up at the cinema one Saturday morning on the pretence that the manager wanted to see me in the projection box.

The box door had a key on the inside as well as a bolt for added security. When I opened the door I found I was locked in with two man-crazy girls bent on a venture that I didn't dare contemplate. What followed was akin to rape: I was held down and semi-stripped, with Veronica squatting on my face whilst Paula made every attempt to get me erect in order to achieve her aim. To say they were rough would be an understatement; it was weeks before the bruises and other marks subsided.

The awful thing was that, as a male, who would have believed me? When they eventually let me go I was quaking with terror. After I got home I hid in my room and wept with the sheer violence and horror of it all. If any man ever doubts the mind-numbing fear most women have of rape, he should go through an experience like that one – then he'd never make light of women's fears again. Later on I learned that Paula was pregnant, and as she had no idea who the father was she'd hoped to set *me* up as the culprit. If she had known me better she could have saved herself a lot of time and me a lot of pain and grief!

But she wasn't prepared to let me off so lightly. Her jokes and comments about me and her continual loud hints about what had not transpired were soon the talk of the cinema, and before long I was summoned to a meeting with one of the senior employees. Alone in his office, sickly anticipating that I was about to get the sack, I was totally unprepared for what happened next. As he started talking about what he had heard he became visibly excited. His breathing grew faster and then he got up from his chair, came round the front of his desk and lunged for my trousers while simultaneously unzipping his own. Rooted to the spot with fear, all I could think of was that if being attacked by two girls had been bad, being attacked by a man would be even worse.

God only knows what would have happened if the cleaner hadn't chosen that very moment to bang on the door. I fled from that room as if I was being pursued by the devil. Somehow I got through the rest of that evening's performance, having locked myself into the projection room, but I knew that when I left that night I would never be able to go back. The moment the show was over I unbolted the door, fled out of the building and rode my scooter to the deserted common. I sat there for hours weeping my heart out, begging God to tell me what was so wrong with me that all these awful things kept happening. When I eventually plucked up the courage to go home I couldn't hide the fact that I had been crying, but I was too bewildered and upset to give my parents any rational explanation for having given up the job they knew I liked so much.

That episode finally made me stop and think about my future. I still couldn't fathom out what was wrong with me or why I should be so different from my peers. The only conclusion I reached was that, despite having enjoyed my eighteen months at the Sellotape laboratory, it was not where I wanted a career.

3
MISSIONARY ZEAL

At seventeen I had just over one year's full-time working experience and two part-time jobs behind me. I'd also had more sexual encounters than most young men of my age could ever dream of.

Although I regularly attended meetings at our church and still accompanied my parents on their missionary work whenever I could, over the years their attitude towards me had developed into one of total perplexity. I'm convinced that in their hearts they really loved me, but they never could approve of me. The main problem was their inability to come to terms with the fact that I couldn't be more like my perfect sister. Though I tried very hard to be the kind of son they wanted me to be, past experience had probably taught them that sooner or later another unforunate escapade would occur to confound and disappoint them yet again.

And who could blame them? After all, they appeared to have all possible reason to imagine that I was as susceptible to the sins of the flesh as every other young adolescent male of my age. Certainly, if the other lads in the neighbourhood viewed my apparent success with girls as a sure sign that I was a budding Casanova, why shouldn't my parents – who believed they had *real* evidence to that effect – share that view? It was ironic when you consider that, now on the threshold of manhood, I was completely convinced that I was hopelessly inadequate when it came to sex, and that my total lack of any normal sexual responses meant that I was never going to be able to live a normal life.

I was about seventeen when I got a job as a costing clerk at the Murphy Chemical Co., just three miles away in the village of Wheathampstead. To my consternation, I found that once again the young women vastly outnumbered the available men. But, having learnt a very painful lesson, this time I decided that if rumours of my sexual inadequacy were not to flourish I would have to be very careful to avoid any situation which might give people cause to speculate.

Now that I was earning more money I was able to part-exchange my Lambretta for a more powerful BSA motorcycle on which I lavished all my pent-up emotion and pride. Each weekend I'd clean and polish it till the chrome sparkled, and frequently I'd strip it right down and clean all its innards so that even the piston and cylinders gleamed like mirrors too. Reluctantly my mother agreed to be my very first passenger, gingerly hitching up her skirts as she hopped aboard the pillion behind me. All went smoothly until I stopped at an intersection and put my feet to the ground. Unfortunately my mother, unsure what to do, decided to emulate me, and when I roared off she was left standing in a decidedly inelegant, legs-akimbo pose in the middle of the road.

That year the Jehovah's Witnesses held a large weekend assembly at Luton Town Football Club. As I'd been asked to help out on all-night security duty, I went straight from work on the Friday evening and reached the ground just in time for the closing sessions of the Assembly. Two other lads and I took turns to snatch the odd hour of sleep in between patrolling the grounds. The following day one of my fellow guards introduced me to a bright, bubbly, young girl with jet-black hair. Sarah stuck by my side, chatting throughout the day until after the evening session when she had to leave.

I'd found Sarah's company pleasant and enjoyable, but that was all. She didn't attract me in the least, and I didn't believe I had given her any encouragment to think otherwise. But, as I very soon found out, I was wrong. I was shaken awake at around two in the morning by one of the guards whispering in a horrified voice that Sarah had somehow managed to get into the grounds and was demanding to know why I hadn't turned up for our prearranged date. Totally mystified, convinced there must have been some mistake. I none the less felt I ought to see the girl and find out what was going on. Anxious to avoid a fuss, I took her to the control box. But no matter how much I asserted that I hadn't arranged a date, Sarah obstinately maintained that I had. In the end, and partly to pacify her, I kissed and cuddled her in the hope that, as a good Jehovah's Witness, she wouldn't be looking for anything more. But I was wrong again, for it soon became clear that Sarah was intent on seduction, and nothing less than total surrender was going to satisfy her.

Once again my ingenuity saved the day and I took refuge in my old stand-by, allowing my tongue to accomplish what other parts couldn't. Thrashing around in a demented frenzy, Sarah finally exploded in an incredibly violent – and incredibly noisy – orgasmic ecstasy that was, at that very moment, also being relayed, courtesy of one of the most sensitive PA systems in the country, to the entire population of Luton! With one of her wild jerks Sarah had switched the machine on. The first we were aware of our unfortunate 'broadcast to the nation' was when we were alerted by the arrival of a breathless, panic-stricken guard begging us to 'get your clothes on and get the hell out of here!' I imagine a new world speed record was set that night for the time it takes two people to get dressed!

Living my life in fear of God's – and my parents' – wrath was by this time an all too familiar state. Since the age of five I had been brought up to believe that God had the power to strike me down should I even think bad thoughts – the fact that I'd not only thought them, but acted upon them and then allowed tens of thousands of local residents to eavesdrop on them, had me quaking in sheer terror. I found myself imagining what horrors awaited me in hell and also, of more immediate significance, what horrors awaited me here on earth when my parents found out the culprit was none other than their very own son. I don't believe I have ever been so scared in my entire life. I couldn't eat, I couldn't sleep (though given the nature of my disturbing dreams, that was a blessing). I didn't even dare leave the house unless it was to go to work or to meetings. It seems to me in retrospect that my life was like a Woody Allen farce: every opportunity was there, but it always led to disaster. I blamed my parents for having brought me up to be unfailingly polite, particularly to women; I blamed Sarah for her stupidity in turning up uninvited, for her determination to seduce me and her mindless thrashing around that had accidentally switched on the PA system; but most of all I blamed myself for being too cowardly to say no. *Why* did these things keep on happening to me? What *was* it about me that attracted all these women so? No matter how many times I asked myself these questions, I never could come up with an answer. Inevitably, each question led me straight back to the most fundamental question of all: What was wrong with me? God's punishment, as it seemed to me then, was not long in arriving.

With my part in 'The Luton Town Incident' still undiscovered, over the next few weeks I gradually regained the confidence to resume my outwardly normal life. Having arranged to meet some friends one evening, I rode my motorbike home from work through torrential rain, stripped off my soaking protective clothing, changed into dry clothes and then dug out an old set of yellow oilskins which I hoped would protect me from the downpour. Travelling out of Harpenden on the A6, I accelerated up to 70 miles per hour along a clear stretch of straight road when, without warning, a van suddenly pulled out of a side turning in front of me. I didn't even have time to brake before I crashed straight into it. My engine stopped dead as the force of the impact buried my treasured bike completely in the van's engine. Still travelling at the same speed, I was propelled 120 feet along the road.

Two things saved me from death or terrible injury. The first was the fact that I had hit a van with a low bonnet, so there was nothing to impede my propulsion; the second was that, as the road was still awash with the torrential rain as I hit the tarmac, I aquaplaned for most of the distance and so prevented massive damage to my body. I recovered consciousness to the sound of horrified whispers.

'I think he's lost his legs,' said one man.

'I don't think he's going to make it,' declared another.

Fortunately, they were both wrong. For 20 agonizing minutes I lay there, unable either to move or to be moved, until an ambulance arrived to take me to St Albans hospital. The police were despatched to notify my shocked parents in the middle of one of their meetings, while I was taken to the theatre so that the surgeon could assess the damage. Two nurses leaned across my body to prevent me seeing the injuries I had sustained while the surgeon carefully cut away the yellow oilskins and the trousers I was wearing beneath. Miraculously, though my legs and feet were badly cut and damaged, no bones were broken. The most difficult and painful task was removing the gravel embedded in my limbs, and in fact I still bear the scars today.

When I was finally sent home, it proved impossible to man-oeuvre the stretcher around the back of the house to my own room. So it was that I spent several weeks confined to bed in my parents' bedroom, a captive audience to their continual ex-hortations to mend my evil ways and do something worthwhile with my life. Privately convinced that my accident had been both a small demonstration of God's wrath and a timely warn-ing, I was physically, emotionally and mentally too wrecked to resist their constant pressurizing any longer.

'What do you want me to do?' I asked weakly.

I should have known what their response would be: 'Follow in your sister's footsteps and become a missionary.'

Desperate to win their approval and prove once and for all that I was not the black sheep of the family, as they so firmly believed, I gave in.

Being a missionary in Leighton Buzzard is probably not as romantic or hazardous as in the Brazilian rainforest but, believe me, it's every bit as onerous – or at least it was for me. For if I'd found a few weekly hours of door-to-door preaching an effort, finding myself committed to a minimum 100 hours of preaching each month in addition to holding down a part-time job in order to support myself was to prove downright gruelling.

As luck would have it, my arrival in Leighton Buzzard coincided with the onset of winter. As I've never been able to tolerate the cold, the sad sight of this freezing individual with blue fingers and a red nose often melted the heart of even the most hardened atheist, so much of my time was spent sipping from a steaming mug of hot chocolate or coffee in the warmth of someone's kitchen.

The problem of where to live was solved by the kindness and generosity of Arthur Howe, the congregation overseer, and his wife Audrey, who offered me a room in their tiny two-up, two-down terraced cottage in the nearby village of Linslade. Arthur and his brother ran an electrical contracting business and, being the selfless, honest and charitable individuals that most Jehovah Witnesses are, they kindly offered me part-time work two days a week. Their offer was all the more generous as my knowledge of electrical wiring was minimal.

If there's one thing I hate more than the cold, it's heights. So you can imagine how I felt when I discovered that most of Arthur's contracting work, rather than being carried out inside buildings, was in fact conducted on top of them. How I managed to conquer my fear and nausea I'll never know, but by some feat I mastered the art of precariously balancing myself at the top of impossibly long ladders and dangerously high gantries without throwing up and falling off – though I have a feeling that this was only accomplished because the sub-zero conditions froze the vomit where it lay in the pit of my stomach! But on the whole my native wit and strong sense of self-preservation enabled me to manoeuvre my two days so adeptly that I only worked on the inside jobs.

The congregation at Leighton Buzzard differed dramatically from the close-knit, harmonious atmosphere I'd enjoyed at Harpenden. I couldn't help but be aware of a marked division of loyalties between those who supported the Howe faction and those who surrounded the Oddie family. As a pioneer I knew I ought to remain neutral, but this proved impossible as I was constantly being invited to different houses on the pretext of sampling one family or another's hospitality – only to find myself subjected to a series of thinly disguised attempts to enrol me in my host's particular 'camp'. Matters weren't helped any by the fact that I lived at Arthur's house and was also employed by his firm.

This precipitated my decision to establish my independence – and therefore my neutrality – by finding myself a bedsitter and self-employed work. Without any capital, it soon became clear that my choices were severely limited. With great ingenuity I acquired a few vital necessities, the lofty title of Plate Glass Restorer and a partner (well, given my fear of heights *someone* had to clean the upstairs windows!), though to be fair 'partner' was a rather grandiose title for Colin, the youth I'd recently met at the local congregation and whom I'd press-ganged into service. Colin was an unusual lad in that he'd become a Jehovah's Witness without any parental encouragement. I often wondered whether he'd joined us more out of a need for friendship than through any religious convictions, particularly when I learned that, though he still lived with his mother (his father had left some years before), she showed no interest in him at all.

As business prospered and Colin and I became reasonably close companions, he seemed to grow more attached to me and to look upon me as his guardian and provider. Despite this, I still managed to keep an evening or two for myself, when I liked to take long, solitary walks along the towpath of the Grand Union Canal, trying to make some sense of the troubled thoughts and emotions that were always lurking in the back of my mind.

I was almost nineteen and yet, no matter how many friends I made or how much company I enjoyed, I still felt incredibly isolated from the rest of the world. Sometimes I wondered half-hopefully whether what I believed to be my life might in reality prove to be nothing more than some terrible nightmare. Thus far, I had to acknowledge, I seemed to have lived with an underlying sense of dream-like unreality. I still dreaded going to bed each night, knowing that 'the dream' was always there, waiting on the edge of sleep to torment me. It had become a nightly ritual for me to tack on to the edge of my prayers a plea to God to release me from the complexities of my situation and allow me to wake up to find that I was just a normal, healthy male. But God consistently failed to hear my pleas.

46

Assemblies are a regular feature in Jehovah's Witness life, and pioneers such as myself were expected to turn up early to lend a helping hand with the preparations. As these events are often attended by visiting congregations from far and wide, a great deal of organization is required in order to provide comfortable accommodation and sufficient food for the faithful thousands who always show up. The obvious commitment and devotion of those who voluntarily donated their time and effort to ensuring that these Assemblies took place with maximum efficiency and minimum fuss never failed to impress me.

It was at one such Assembly that I met Olive, a fellow pioneer from Seven Sisters in London, who made no bones about the fact that she was immensely attracted to me. It was hardly surprising when you considered the shortage of eligible males in our organization coupled with the ruling that strictly prohibited fraternization with 'outsiders'. One might think that my earlier disastrous experiences would have set the alarm bells ringing, but an in-built reluctance to offend made it difficult for me to reject Olive's determined advances. And so, with growing dismay, over the next few months I found myself gradually but relentlessly backed into a siding by an overwhelmingly powerful engine.

First I was paraded in front of her parents, whose indulgent smiles and approving nods were the first warning sign. Then I was shown off to her envious friends, whose unsubtle winks and coy comments were the second. By the time Olive got round to broaching the subject of marriage, even this cowardly character didn't need a third. But she turned out to be the kind of girl who was not prepared to take rejection lying down and, after all her tears and tantrums and threats had failed to achieve the desired effect, she promptly mounted a campaign with all the military precision of a seasoned soldier in an attempt to enlist my parents help in changing my mind.

I found the whole experience so unnerving that I realized I had no alternative but to keep all women forever at arm's length. But it was so difficult. I loved their company. I enjoyed their conversation. I so desperately wanted to be good friends with them, but for some strange reason platonic relationships with me seemed to be the last thing on their minds. And so it was that regretfully, though determinedly, I resolved to have nothing further to do with them.

Until I met Susannah. My first inauspicious encounter with her occurred when my resolve to live a blameless life was still burning. I was standing on the doorstep of an ordinary prefabricated, chalet-style house preaching to the lady who had answered my knock at the door when I caught sight of a pretty girl who kept shyly peering, then disappearing around the edge of a door. I thought no more about the incident until a few weeks later when I was walking home from a meeting. Suddenly, from out of nowhere, Susannah stepped in front of me and asked whether I was the same person who had called upon her mother. When I acknowledged that I was, we fell into an easy, friendly conversation and I walked her home.

Over the next few weeks Susannah seemed to pop up miraculously wherever I went. The significance of her frequent appearances, alone and always at night ,was not lost on me, but as she'd never made any overt moves I was happy to pass time in her company. It became a habit for me to see her safely home and so, little by little, I learned more about her and the difficult life she had led.

Susannah, who lived alone with her partially disabled mother, had suffered greatly at the hands of a sadistic father who had beaten her frequently and severely throughout her childhood. All my chivalrous instincts were aroused as I began to understand why, despite her age, she still seemed little more than a frightened, shy child. So I allowed our harmless friendship to continue, safe in the knowledge that Susannah didn't have a scheming bone in her body.

When Susannah's mother issued an invitation to tea I eagerly accepted, anticipating a pleasant, undemanding evening and better food than I was used to. During the meal, however, when Susannah had popped out of the room, her mother suddenly turned to me and said, 'Susannah's very keen on you, Keith.'

Not knowing how to reply, I merely smiled and stuffed another piece of her delicious home-made cake into my mouth.

'And I just want you to know that I ...er, *approve*,' she continued pointedly.

At first I wasn't sure what she could possibly mean. What, precisely, did she approve of? And then it began to dawn on me. At that point I thought it would be best if I made my escape.

'Good heavens, is that the time? I really must be off.' I responded nervously.

'You can't go yet – it's far too early,' Susannah's mother quickly replied. 'Besides, Susannah's just made another cup of tea.'

Another half-hour passed as we sat round the table drinking

more tea. Susannah and her mother kept exchanging meaningful looks, and I was beginning to feel more uncomfortable with each passing minute. Several times I stood up with an excuse to leave, but each time I was thwarted by their apparent determination that I should stay. Then Susannah's mother spoke, and what she said numbed my brain so completely I couldn't think of anything to say.

'Why don't you two go off to bed and leave me to clear up down here?'

Though she put it as a question, it was more like an order. Panic began to rise in me. Should I stay? Should I go? Would they *let* me go? What possible valid reason could I give for leaving? I didn't live with anybody. I had no one waiting up for me at home. No one even knew where I was! It may sound a weak excuse, but I was in such a state of shock that I just gave in and meekly followed Susannah up the stairs. I'd been in unusual situations with girls before. I'd even been caught red-handed with a girl before. But nothing had ever prepared me for a situation like this. Not only was Susannah's mother condoning this fiasco – she was actively encouraging it!

Nervously, I undressed and slipped between the sheets of Susannah's bed. She had a beautiful body: her skin was so white it almost seemed translucent, and her long dark hair, which trailed across her breasts, was soft and silky enough to drive any man wild. But all I could think of was how much I envied her, and, lovely as she was, I knew I couldn't make love to her. At the same time, there was something so shy, so appealing and so vulnerable about Susannah that I couldn't possibly do anything to hurt her.

I decided the only way out was to confess. I pulled Susannah into my arms and, without daring to look her in the eye, whispered into her ear everything I felt she had a right to know. I had no idea how she would react. Half of me anticipated that she would laugh, while the other half expected her to be angry. Instead, she cried – not out of a sense of rejection, but with real sympathy for my plight. It was then that she confided more about her own past to me. Her father had not just beaten her but had sexually abused her too. We lay there throughout the night, taking it in turns to weep and comfort each other, knowing that we both had serious problems. In the morning we had breakfast with her mother, who seemed rather pleased with what she thought she had accomplished, and then I left.

I wouldn't have blamed Susannah if she had never wanted to

see me again, but I desperately hoped that she would, for I felt I had at last found a soulmate. Three long and lonely days passed, during which there was no contact. Just as I was beginning to resign myself to the fact that Susannah was probably laughing behind my back – as so many girls had done before – she reappeared, to accost me once more in the street.

'Come home with me, Keith,' she pleaded.

I agreed, but first I insisted on dropping my bag off at home. Somehow, taking my Bible along to this kind of assignation just didn't seem right.

Susannah's mother was busy preparing supper. When we sat down to the meal she suddenly looked at me closely and I froze as she said, 'Susannah's been telling me about your problem.' Unsure whether I had unwittingly offered myself up as a victim for humiliation or, worse still, blackmail, I just sat rooted to the spot, waiting for the other shoe to drop. She then proceeded to explain to me how difficult it had been for Susannah to form any normal relationships because of the way her father had used her.

'You're a nice young man, Keith. As soon as I met you I could see you would be perfect for Susannah. And now that I know all about your own problems, I'm convinced you can both help each other to lead a normal life.'

The sense of unreality I'd always lived with deepened over the next few months as I tried desperately to develop a normal, satisfactory relationship with Susannah. And always there was her mother, encouraging us and trying to help with her cool, calm, analytical discussions of our mutual problems.

At the same time, the situation within the congregation was getting worse as the rift between the two warring factions grew wider and more bitter each week. The pressures of being stuck in the middle of the Howes and the Oddies each evening as well as trying to please Susannah and her mother inevitably began to take their toll. My pioneering work, which I'd undertaken with such zeal, had, like everything I seemed to do, degenerated into farce.

Rescue came in the form of the circuit overseer who, by now well aware of the huge divide in the Leighton Buzzard congregation, ordered me back home to Harpenden. I took my leave of a tearful Susannah and her even more regretful mother with much sadness and many promises to keep in touch. But I think we all knew that it would be far too painful to keep those promises. Looking back now, I can see how some moralists might decry what Susannah's mother did, but I truly believe that she had her daughter's best interests at heart. As for Susannah, I can only hope that this sweet, kind, caring, unselfish girl has found happiness with a sensitive, gentle and patient man who has been able to eradicate the nightmares of what she suffered at her father's hands.

So I returned home to Harpenden with another failure behind me to add to the growing store of disappointments I could read in my parents' eyes. With no job, no money and no real skills to offer, I did the only thing I could. I took an early morning job helping out at the local newsagent's where I'd been a paper boy in my youth. Seven days a week I'd get up at four-thirty, mark up forty-five newspaper rounds and then help the paper boys and girls disperse their hefty bundles throughout the town and rural areas. I was supplied with a van – a decrepit one to be sure, but to me it was sheer luxury because it meant that at least I now had wheels. When the steering wheel came adrift from the drive shaft while I was out on my rounds one day, I thought for one awful moment that my time was up. Helplessly I waited for the almighty impact that was sure to follow as the van slowly mounted the pavement and demolished a lamp post which, in excruciating slow motion, folded in half and came to rest on top of the van. Fortunately I escaped without injury, and as soon as the state of the van was discovered it was immediately replaced by a smart new one which proudly proclaimed 'Whitehouse's' in the freshly painted livery colours of the shop.

Whitehouse's was part of a chain of five shops owned by Councillor Ken Hill, who at that time was Mayor of St Albans. Councillor Hill was a kind and a generous employer who allowed me to assume as much responsibility as I could cope with, culminating in promotion to joint manager. My co-manager, Miss Culley, and I worked well together, and over the two years I spent there we were so successful that we were able to add records to the existing lines of gifts, tobacco and stationery. One of our more famous customers was a Mr Freddie Bartholomew, otherwise known as the wonderfully funny Eric Morecambe. When we used some of our profits to splash out on a refurbishment of the shop, I boldly asked Mr Bartholomew if he would preside over the Grand Reopening. It never occurred to me that celebrities could (and invariably did) charge enormous fees for such appearances, and to his eternal credit Eric never saw fit to enlighten me. But that was typical of the man, who was as genuinely nice in private as he was in public.

The work was hard and the days were long, but for the first

time in my life I was, if not happy, at least far too busy to concentrate on my own problems. In addition, as I had very little time for social life I was able – with one or two minor exceptions – to avoid repeating any of my former abysmal failures with the local girls. But even those exceptions turned out to be not quite as bad as I had feared. The first occurred when one of the female employees made a misguided play for me; fortunately I was able to deflect it on the basis that it was unwise to mix business with pleasure. The second proved to be more difficult to extricate myself from with the same degree of dignity, but by now I was becoming so inured to being the object of derision that, outwardly at least, I was able to pretend I didn't care.

Inwardly, however, each failure cut just as deep as the last. It is an eternal puzzle why I allowed myself to be drawn into these situations. Part of me obviously hoped that *this time* things might be different. But it never was. The fact is, my life seemed to me to be like a badly scripted B movie filmed in black and white, while everyone else was experiencing the real thing in colour.

Things were slightly different when Lucy, whose brother had nearly killed me with his runaway motorbike some years before, re-entered my life. Lucy was a very unusual girl who, apart from being enormous fun and an outrageous flirt, was also refreshingly frank. But what made her unique in my experience was the fact that she lacked any sense of shame or embarrassment. For some reason Lucy latched on to me and, welcoming the light relief, I did nothing to discourage her friendship.

Because I started work so early in the morning I kept odd hours throughout the day. This meant that I had one and a half hours' break between nine and ten-thirty, when I'd go home for breakfast, and another break between one and three-thirty in the afternoon for lunch. Taking advantage of the fact that my father was at work all day and my mother was also out for most of the time, Lucy very quickly adopted the habit of popping in and out of our house on occasions when I was at home alone.

Naturally it didn't take long for Lucy to uncover the truth about me, but unlike all her predecessors she simply chose to ignore it. She would frequently have me on the verge of an apoplectic fit when she innocently made some remark in front of my parents that had me convinced she was on the point of blurting out an incriminating detail about the various intimacies we indulged in. Although she always stopped short, I lived in constant fear that one day she just might reveal all. In fact, though Lucy caused me so many heart-stopping moments of fear, I was filled with admiration for her nerve. She'd think nothing of interrupting me while I was in the middle of decorating our bathroom and calmly stripping off to take a bath – apparently oblivious to any thought of my mother walking in. And on the few occasions when my mother did come home – while we were both in my bed, I might add – she'd simply throw on her clothes, perch herself on the bed and greet my mother as sweetly and nonchalantly as you please!

Despite Lucy's brazenness, I couldn't help being drawn by her apparently irrepressible sense of fun; and though she was far from being the brightest of girls, her naïvety and straightforwardness endeared her to me. Perhaps those characteristics endeared her to my parents as well, for the one thing I could never quite work out was why, when they had ample justification for regarding me as the local stud, for some strange reason they never displayed the slightest shred of suspicion about our friendship. By coincidence she later married one of my cousins, but, unfortunately, it didn't last very long.

Wednesdays were the only night I had off, and these I spent in the West End seeing a show or film with a (platonic) girlfriend. On our way home we'd stop off at the Golden Dragon Chinese restaurant for a meal, and then round the evening off by going upstairs to the Nine-Ten Gambling Club to watch the punters lose their money. It was on one of these occasions that I got chatting to the owner of the club and learned that he owned a large house which he wanted to let. I was earning a great deal of money for a young man my age – which, I realized, enabled me to seize this opportunity to make even more: I leased the house from him and then promptly sub-let it as four flats. I already had my first tenant lined up in the shape of Dulcie, my friendly local traffic warden, and I didn't believe it would be too difficult to find another three.

Unfortunately my friendship with Dulcie, a divorced women of around thirty-five, was misinterpreted by my father, who caused a terribly embarrassing confrontation when he refused to believe that I wasn't 'keeping an older woman', as he'd heard. The arguments between Dad and myself on this issue produced a lot of tension between us, and our relationship, which had never been good even at the best of times, began to deteriorate further. It upset me greatly that Dad and I seemed to have such difficulty in developing the kind of relationship I had always wanted and needed. Sometimes I felt as though we were becoming close, only to find it all disappear again.

One occasion that does stand out in my memory as a time when I felt very close to my father was when, as the proud owner of an ancient Austin 16 car which I had recently acquired for the princely sum of £25, I took him and my mother on holiday to Wales. Dad was in his element as he navigated, choosing secondary, and even unclassified, roads that took us through pretty countryside. The car coped well with the bumpy terrain as we climbed a steep, unclassified road, and when we had successfully negotiated the summit to start our descent she began to pick up speed at a cracking pace. Unfortunately, older vehicles had a tendency to suffer from 'brake fade' when the brake drums became overheated, and to counter this I was forced to change right down into first gear, apply the foot brake and even the hand brake.

Meanwhile, Mum was chattering away in the back seat, blissfully unaware of the fact that, despite all my efforts, we were still picking up speed. Dad and I exchanged a silent look of panic when, as we neared the bottom of the incline, a sharp bend loomed in front of us. There was only one thing left: I had to steer the car at a slight angle in the hope that hitting the chain link fence along the roadside would hold the car firm and, I hoped, push it around the bend. The mudguard hit the fence with a thud, then scraped along with a harsh metallic sound. Miraculously the fence held, we made it round the bend and gradually came to a halt several hundred yards further along.

'Now's as good a time as any to stop for a while to give the brakes a chance to cool down,' Dad wisely advised. While we were waiting I walked back up the road to take a look at the spot which had caused us so much concern. I wondered whether I would have had the courage to take such a gamble with our lives if I had known that beyond that chain link fence lay a forty-foot drop!

Despite our brush with disaster we had a wonderful touring holiday, staying in bed and breakfasts, relaxing and doing things together that we normally never had the time or opportunity to do at home. For one of the very few times in my life I felt as if we were just like every other ordinary family, and though, sadly, the feeling was not to last, the memory of that holiday in Wales is one I will treasure forever.

When we returned home the distance between Dad and me returned also, and as it became more and more intolerable I began to realize that it was time I bought my own home. It was while looking around for a suitable property that Vivienne popped up again in my life. I was in the shop one day when she appeared, obviously deeply distressed. It wasn't hard to work out why. Vivienne was in a very advanced stage of pregnancy. Apparently her parents had thrown her out and, having nowhere to go, for some strange reason she had decided to come to me.

By now I had let all the flats in the house I was leasing, so that option was closed. However, vulnerable women have always managed to bring out the soft side in me, and so I came up with the bright idea of temporarily installing her in the room above the shop while I worked out what to do. For three days and nights Vivienne slept, if not in comfort then in blissful contentment, certain that good old Keith would come up with a solution to her problem. Meanwhile, I spent three sleepless nights trying to work out what to do – in between worrying what would happen if Mr Hill and my parents discovered what was going on. I found Vivienne temporary accommodation, provided her with money for food and rent, and spent endless hours worrying about her plight. I even took her to the hospital when she went into labour (protesting my innocence to the midwives all the while), and then took it upon myself to visit the mother and inform her of the arrival of her new grandchild.

To my relief and surprise, Vivienne's mother seemed to accept this fact with some resignation. She merely said: 'Oh, well, you'd better tell her to come back home when she gets out – and bring her bastard with her.' Apparently this was the second of what was to become Vivienne's large illegitimate brood, each by a different father; and on each occasion the scenario of being thrown out, only to be taken back into the family fold after the birth, was to be repeated. They were a strange family. But I'd done my duty, and now all I wanted was to wash my hands of the whole affair.

With dramas like that, it wasn't surprising that I soon had the added worry of losing my hair. I spent a small fortune on visits to a hair treatment clinic in Luton, and though on each subsequent visit I was assured that there was a definite improvement, I continued to part with both hair and money. I became more and more depressed at this time, not just because of my rapidly thinning hair, but because there seemed to be so little to look forward to in my life. I had a good job which paid exceedingly well, and I'd even managed to put down a deposit on a small house, but none of these accomplishments was sufficient compensation for the fact that in every *real* respect my life was in a hopeless mess. My parents were baffled and deeply disappointed with me, every girl I met inevitably became frustrated and disillusioned with me, and even God Himself must be offended because he still refused to hear my tearful nightly pleas. Somehow, it seemed as if the harder I tried to please, the more I ended up displeasing. There had to be some way of getting my life in order and of making my parents proud of their son.

My mood was so desperate that, when I bumped into Margaret Oakley again, it seemed a good idea to pick up our relationship where it had left off. After all, Margaret was a sweet girl who was not only comfortable to be with but still shy enough not to think it odd if I made no sexual moves; and, equally important, she was a good Jehovah's Witness of whom my parents would wholeheartedly approve. Thus we embarked on a fairly easy courtship that everyone assumed would some day end in marriage, and for the first time in my life I actually began to experience some sense of calm.

Had I but known it, that calm was to precede an almighty storm. For that was the moment God finally chose to hear my pleas and send me Marylin.

4
FIRST LOVE

I was working out my notice with Councillor Hill, eagerly anticipating the training course I would soon be going on to prepare me for my new job as a sales representative with Hoover Ltd. In need of small change for the shop, I popped along to the bank with a bundle of notes. 'Five pounds' worth of florins, five of half crowns, and five each of shillings and sixpences,' I said to the girl behind the counter, as I counted out notes to the value of £20. Then I looked up.

The breath caught in my throat as I looked straight into the eyes of the most beautiful girl I had ever seen. And I was totally unprepared for the wave of curious sensations that swept over me as she stared straight back into my eyes.

'Sorry, could you repeat that?' She apologized with a smile.

'Um, er... a tenner's worth of ten bob notes... er, a fiver's worth of coppers and... um, I'll take the rest in sixpences,' I replied falteringly, unable to take my eyes off her face.

I left the bank in a complete daze. It was only when I looked at the pile of wrong coins and notes that I hadn't realized I'd asked for that I began to feel foolish. Half-hoping, half-fearing to see the beautiful new cashier again, I made another trip to the bank. I didn't know whether to feel glad or disappointed when I saw someone else in her place. This time I emerged with the correct change and the rubber stamp the bank allowed me to borrow to enable me to save time by pre-stamping the paying-in slips for the deposits I would be making that night.

When I arrived back at the shop, Doug, our representative from Pye records, was standing on the pavement outside waiting to speak to me. Although married, Doug was a self-confessed womanizer and, having no one else he could safely confide in, we had a standing arrangement to have lunch at Le Capri whenever he called so that he could bring me up to date on his latest exploits. As we stood there on the pavement, chatting, a voice suddenly interrupted us.

'I understand you've stolen my rubber stamp.' When I turned round I was face to face with the beautiful girl from the bank.

She was about five feet seven with long, dark hair, a shapely body and, judging by her jutting chin and challenging smile, a personality and strength of character that were remarkable in one so young. And once again I found myself faltering for words.

Assessing the situation, smoothie Doug took control. 'We're just going for lunch at Le Capri. Why don't you join us?' he invited.

To my surprise, she agreed. Throughout the lunch, Marylin and Doug kept up a line in humorous banter, while all I could do was sit and stare wordlessly at Marylin and wonder at the strength of the attraction I felt for her. It was the first time in my life I had experienced such a strong – and profound – attraction towards a girl.

I couldn't get her out of my mind. All I could think about for the rest of the day and night was how I could meet her again. The following day I was a nervous wreck. I had to see Marylin again, but how? Working up my courage, I waited until it was almost lunchtime and then nervously went along to the bank on the pretext of requiring change. I tried so hard to appear to be cool and casual, but I was shaking so much that my words fell over themselves without making any sense. Calmly Marylin waited, a little smile hovering at the corner of her mouth.

'Will you ... I mean, er, would you like to come to Le Capri for lunch again?' I eventually managed to blurt out. To my surprise and delight she agreed to meet me fifteen minutes later. My feet fairly flew back down the street as, heart thumping to an unfamiliar beat, I contemplated the exciting prospect of spending a whole, uninterrupted hour in the company of Marylin and wondering whether this heart-stopping, ecstatic feeling that was so foreign could possibly be love?

With each passing minute that we lingered in Le Capri I became more and more enthralled. Hesitantly, I asked: 'Would you like to take a look at the house I'm in the process of buying?'

She seemed impressed and smiled her agreement. As we drove to my new house I jokingly commented that, though I'd had lots of offers of help, I still had no one to make my new curtains for me. 'So how are you at sewing?' I laughed. On the return drive I plucked up the courage to ask her if she would have dinner with me that night – to which, once again, she agreed. I couldn't believe it? That this beautiful girl wanted to go out with me was incredible.

I was so excited, I couldn't wait for the evening to come. The moment I finished work, I rushed straight home and scoured the Yellow Pages in search of a restaurant special enough for such a wonderful girl.

Marylin lived in Wheathampstead with her grandmother, with whom she had stayed ever since her mother had returned to her home town of Torquay following the tragic death of Marylin's father in a road accident three years earlier. The grandmother was a sweet old lady but, as I soon found out, Marylin's mother was a different kettle of fish. Having been brought up with the idea that women should never work, she had married an army officer while she was still very young and had then been thoroughly spoiled with servants and a comfortable, easy lifestyle when he was posted to Berlin. Naturally her husband's death had come as a terrible shock to Marylin's mother and, unable to cope, she had had a nervous breakdown and spent some time in a mental institution. When she recovered she passed much of her time in the company of other men, leaving Marylin alone at home to look after her two younger sisters. Eventually she moved to Torquay, taking the two younger girls with her and leaving Marylin to live with her grandmother.

I took Marylin to dinner at the Cowper Arms at Digswell, near Welwyn Garden City. Wanting everything to be perfect I spared no expense, ordering the finest food as though I'd done it a thousand times before. Perusing the wine list, I nonchalantly added: 'And bring us a bottle of Nuits St George.' It wasn't until weeks later (after we were married, in fact) that Marylin teasingly told me that I had mispronounced it as 'Noots St George'.

Just one evening with her was enough to convince me that for the first time in my life I was totally, incredibly and irrevocably in love. What was even more amazing was that Marylin appeared to feel the same way, too! Immediately I did the honourable thing by breaking off my relationship with Margaret. From that moment on, I intended to spend every available moment with Marylin.

The change in my life and my personality were dramatic. The nightmare that had haunted my sleeping hours for so long suddenly seemed to be nothing more than an irritating, albeit recurring, bad dream which ceased to torment me the moment I awoke to thoughts of Marylin. The miracle of love had come into my life, and I was determined that nothing was ever going to be allowed to dim the wonder and joy of this precious gift.

Marylin and I saw each other at every possible opportunity, and our mutual love grew stronger daily. I would leave romantic little notes in the basket of her bicycle when she was at work, send her soppy little cards, and buy her flowers and silly, inexpensive little gifts. All my romantic impulses that had for so long been stifled now had an outlet, and I couldn't help expressing all the love and happiness that were bubbling up inside me.

On 5 November 1967, just ten short days after we had met, as the night sky exploded with the shooting stars of fireworks celebrating the anniversary of Guy Fawkes' attempt to blow up the Houses of Parliament, the stark black and white imagery of my previously monochrome life exploded into glorious, living colour as I placed an engagement ring on Marylin's finger. The only dreams I had that night were of Marylin. The nightmare had gone and I was finally free.

Unbelievable as it might seem, throughout our brief courtship sex never once entered my mind. Everything had happened so quickly, and we were so caught up in our plans, that there was little enough time even to think, let alone worry about sex or the prospect of failure. The only worries I had were to do with my parents' reaction.

Just as I had feared, when I broke the news to Mum and Dad they flew into a terrible rage. My defection from Margaret was bad enough, but that I should display so little regard for our religion as to consider committing one of its most cardinal sins – that was too much for God to forgive. As they pleaded with me to change my mind, I wept. They tried begging; I tried explaining. Then they tried threatening, but their threats only hardened my resolve. When they issued an ultimatum, I knew I had no choice. For the first – the only – time in my life I was in love, and although I tried my utmost to make them understand, the depth of my feeling for Marylin was incomprehensible to them. How *could* they understand? They'd never known about the long years of misery and self-doubt that I had endured, so why should I expect them to understand now? Their attitude was inflexible, their devotion to their religion total: to marry outside of the religion was to forfeit all hope of everlasting life. With tears streaming down my face I packed a few essentials in a bag and left my childhood home. Though I'd never known complete happiness there, it *was* my home and, despite everything, I loved my parents very much.

As my own house was not quite ready to move into, Marylin's

grandmother allowed me to stay with them. In a week's time I would be joining Hoover, and as I'd left Whitehouse's the week before I had seven whole days in which to enjoy Marylin's company before I had to go away on my residential training course.

As luck would have it, both Marylin and I caught severe colds and that precious week, for which we had made so many plans, was spent in bed – she in hers, I in mine, for Marylin's grandmother was a vigilant guardian who viewed an engagement ring as a poor excuse for letting down her guard. But we were young and in love, and luck was on our side. When Marylin's grandmother was out shopping one day, and with no other motive than a discussion of our wedding plans, I joined Marylin in her room. One thing inevitably led to another, and before I knew what was happening we were making tender, passionate love. Afterwards, cuddling Marylin in my arms, I felt as if I was walking on air. *There's nothing wrong with me, after all*, I thought triumphantly. *All I needed was to meet the right girl.* I was so happy I could hardly speak. The truth was, no words could possibly describe what I was feeling and when the thought occurred: *My God, what would I have done if I had never met Marylin?* I could only cling on to her and hold her tightly, knowing that it would be impossible for me ever to let her go.

When I heard footsteps on the path I had difficulty tearing myself away from Marylin's side, but knowing how outraged her grandmother would be if she caught us in bed together I had no choice. With a foolish grin of pure joy I crept back to my bed.

I couldn't believe it. It was incredible! A miracle! I was twenty-one years of age and I'd finally become a man! I wanted to throw open the window and proclaim my joy to the world. Every single emotion and thought I'd ever read about or seen in the movies coursed through my veins. I wanted to sing it from the mountain tops and shout it from the chimney stacks. I was in love ... and I had just *made* love – and all with the woman of my dreams!

With my four-week course looming, we made as many plans as we could. We'd originally planned to get married in March 1968, but now we both knew we couldn't wait that long, so we brought the date forward to 6 January. Meanwhile there was so much to do. I telephoned Marylin's mother and formally asked for her daughter's hand, invitations were sent out, Doug agreed to be my best man, and Auntie Elsie and Uncle Ray said they'd be delighted to come. But from my parents there was no word.

With most of the arrangements made, I tore myself away from Marylin's side and set off for Watford to start training for my new career. Now, more than ever, I was determined to build a successful life for Marylin and, of course, the children we hoped to have straightaway. Despite missing Marylin dreadfully, I acquitted myself well on the arduous course. Every aspect of salesmanship was covered, and when we weren't attending lectures and seminars on selling techniques we'd be locked in sessions specifically designed to help us assimilate what we had learned. It was during one of these sessions that I was called away to take an urgent phone call that had come through. It was Marylin. She was panic-stricken because my mother had visited her at the bank and asked her to call round at my parents' house that night. I was horrified. What were Mum and Dad up to now? Knowing I couldn't possibly allow Marylin to face them alone, I begged my instructor to release me for the evening on compassionate grounds, saying that there was an emergency at home.

I drove like a maniac to Harpenden to collect Marylin, and together we presented ourselves at my parents' front door. Though they must have been surprised to see me there, neither of them let it show. I held fast to Marylin's hand, willing her not to allow them to intimidate her and bravely trying to hide my mounting fear. We sat down on the settee like polite strangers, waiting for my father to speak. When he did, he took the wind right out of my sails.

'Are you pregnant?' he asked Marylin. I was so appalled and ashamed that I hardly knew what to say.

'Of course she's not,' I protested. 'Please try to understand. We love each other very much and, though we hate to see you both so unhappy, we *will* be married. There's nothing either of you can say or do to make us change our minds."

'You seem like a nice enough girl,' my father said to Marylin. 'And it's not that we've got anything against you personally. It's just that. . . .' He stopped, too upset to go on as the tears trickled down his face. I knew what my parents were thinking. Their attitude might seem strange to anyone not brought up in such a rigid religion, but I understood what they were going through. Their devotion to their faith was total. My father was an Elder, and the church meant a great deal to him. My mother was even more fanatically devoted than he was, and I don't believe it's an exaggeration to say that she would have died for her beliefs.

Poor Marylin could only stand and stare at the three of us as the tears poured down our cheeks. It was hardly the best circumstances in which to meet my parents for the first time, and I'm sure she was totally nonplussed. I was devastated, but part of me could only admire their absolute refusal to compromise. Being a Jehovah's Witness is not easy – in fact, it's probably one of the hardest religions to follow. But my parents were committed so wholeheartedly that they really believed they were doing the right thing. They couldn't give us their blessing, and we refused to cancel our plans. Eventually, knowing there was nothing more I could say or do, Marylin and I took our leave. We didn't see my parents again until after the wedding.

We spent Christmas at Torquay with Marylin's family. At first her mother and I got on well (though time was to alter that in the same way that it's altered so many things in my life), and I thoroughly enjoyed the first *real* Christmas I had known since religion entered my life. January came, and our long-awaited day finally dawned. I had spent the night before at my Auntie Kath's, unable to sleep through nervousness, still praying that at the last moment my parents would relent and show up at the reception. Doug and I looked resplendent in top hat and tails. Auntie Kath had wisely forced a brandy down my throat to still my knocking knees, but I was shaking right up to the moment when I saw Marylin walk down the aisle. She looked so radiant that she took my breath away.

We spent eight glorious days honeymooning in London, seeing the sights, taking in the shows and, of course, making love. We acted like kids let loose on a spree. We played silly games with each other, saw cartoon films galore, even played games of hopscotch in the street. We didn't mind that we couldn't afford to eat in the hotel – we were happy enough with sandwiches, hot dogs and burgers bought from street stalls. All that mattered was that we were hopelessly in love.

We stayed with Marylin's grandmother until March when we were finally able to move into our first home at 14 Westfield Drive, the very same house about which I once joked that Marylin might like to make the curtains. Having cut my income by two-thirds when I'd moved to Hoover, the additional expenses of the wedding and the house purchase meant we were now broke, but we didn't mind in the least. And when Marylin told me she was pregnant, we had even more cause to rejoice. I fussed around her like an old woman. There was nothing I loved more than cooking and cleaning the house and when, three months into the pregnancy, the doctor informed us that Marylin was carrying twins, it provided me with the perfect excuse to envelop her with even more love. I think that was possibly the happiest year of my life. I'd spend hours lying in bed next to Marylin, my head close to her stomach, one hand resting protectively on top as I heard and felt our babies moving inside.

When my sons were born I was with Marylin throughout. Though it was a difficult labour, the moment Stephen emerged I was filled with so much emotion I thought I would choke. As Andrew was not to arrive for another two hours, I was allowed plenty of time to hold Stephen in my arms. My elation was indescribable, for no words can do justice to that incredible feeling of having helped to create not one, but two, new lives. Having had two forceps deliveries Marylin was exhausted, and as she fell asleep I held her hand and gazed lovingly at my two sons. If anyone had ever had cause to doubt my manhood, what Marylin and I had accomplished together must surely now have confounded them all. We experienced a few traumatic days when Stephen was rushed off to St Albans Hospital with stomach problems, which fortunately turned out not to be too serious and soon he was returned to us and I was able to take my wife and sons home to Harpenden.

I had taken a substantial drop in salary when I joined Hoover, and now the strain that Andrew and Stephen put on our already stretched finances meant that I had to take on extra work. So after a full day's work I did a part-time job as a barman from six till eleven, as well as a gardening job that occupied one whole day each weekend. But I was never happier or more fulfilled, particularly as the twins' birth had prompted a reconciliation with Mum and Dad who, having been presented with a *fait accompli*, now concentrated all their efforts on saving my soul by converting Marylin. They never did succeed, but when the twins arrived they were so smitten with their grandsons that they couldn't possibly bring themselves to reject any of us again. Besides, their faith was strong and I'm sure they believed it was only a matter of time.

Most men find fatherhood a wonderful experience but for me it was far, far more than that. I revelled in every lovely, grubby, sticky, messy moment of it – even to the point of changing dirty nappies, which is often the point at which some men's willingness to muck in comes to an abrupt halt. To bath my sons and watch them gurgle with delight as they splashed around in the water was a constant delight, and although for most of their waking hours (and many of their sleeping hours, too) I would be out of the house earning the money to support us all, back home I was never too tired to spend time cuddling or feeding them. If meeting Marylin had brought peace and contentment into my life, becoming a father had increased that feeling a thousand-fold.

Although I worked hard at Hoover, winning prizes and competitions for the best salesman over and over again, I wasn't particularly popular with my colleagues. It took me a long time to realize that I had joined a company that had grown fat with complacency and my efforts were making everyone else look bad. It wasn't that I was necessarily better than everyone else, but my ambition to do well fired me with enthusiasm and, having read Victor Kiam's autobiography, I had come to believe that if you're prepared to work twice as long and twice as hard as everyone else you can't help but come out on top.

I never mixed with my colleagues after work because I just didn't have the spare cash to buy myself or them a drink. The mortgage was crippling us, and we were so hard up that we'd often go without things ourselves at the end of the month to enable the boys to have everything they needed. But when you're young and in love you survive the hard times, and though juggling work and my part-time jobs was exhausting, I always seemed to find the energy to keep going.

Less than two years later, Marylin was expecting again. We were overjoyed and very much hoped that this time we would have a daughter to make our family complete. Naturally we anticipated that everybody else would share our happiness, but when we broke the news to Mum and Dad, who openly adored Stephen and Andrew, their disapproval and hostility took us aback.

'It's wrong to bring more children into such a wicked world,' they preached at us, 'particularly when the Bible tells us that those who are evil will soon be destroyed by God!' I was so incensed by their negative attitude that for once I couldn't stop myself from arguing.

'How dare you tell us what we should do,' I protested. 'No one has the right to dictate to us how many children we should have, or when.'

I just couldn't believe their attitude, and this time my anger lasted for weeks. Eventually, of course, they got used to the fact, and on the surface at least the rift was once more breached. Ironically, when my sister Pearl (ten years older than I and with two young teenagers to boot) announced shortly afterwards that she was expecting twins, my parents greeted *her* news with a great show of pleasure and a noted absence of adverse comment. Despite all the treasures I now had in my life, I still craved my parents' approval, and their obvious preference for Pearl hurt every bit as much as it had done when I was a boy.

Marylin's second pregnancy didn't go well. In her sixth month she was confined to bed with a threatened miscarriage, and having to look after two little boys, hold down two part-time jobs as well as a full-time job and care for a sick, pregnant wife in addition to dealing with all the cooking and cleaning left me exhausted. But nothing was too good for my Marylin and I fussed around her like a mother hen, always finding the time to do special, romantic little things like placing flowers on her dinner tray and devizing tasty little recipes for her. I remember the day she had a yen for something sweet. All I could find in the kitchen was a packet of Angel Delight. As I whisked it up with milk in a bowl and watched it turn bright green, I felt quite proud of my culinary ability. I sat on the bed, grinning with pleasure at the expression on Marylin's face as she ate it all, right down to the very last spoonful – blissfully ignorant of the fact that what I had taken for a smile was, in reality, a grimace of distaste. Poor Marylin – to this day she cannot stand the sight of green Angel Delight! It also makes me smile now when I think about the midwife who used to call round to check up on Marylin's progress. How it used to amuse her to see me struggling with a baby under each arm and a vacuum cleaner in one hand. 'You know,' she said to me once, 'you'd make someone a wonderful wife.' I often wonder what she would say if she could see me now!

However, when Rebecca Louise was finally born on 1 April 1971, Marylin and I had to agree that all the work and the worry had been well worth it. Her birth coincided with my promotion to area manager, a position which carried a salary substantial enough not only to ease our financial burden but also to allow us to move to a larger house. We found just what we were looking for in a small village called Langford, just three miles south-west of Biggleswade in Bedfordshire. It was a modern, three-bedroom detached house that boasted a separate lounge, dining room and study, and on the day we moved in I couldn't help feeling proud of my achievements.

The horrors and the self-doubt that had characterized my former life were little more than a vague memory now. I had a successful career which I enjoyed, a wonderful, loving wife and three beautiful, perfect children. I may have considered myself a failure as a boy, but meeting Marylin had, I felt, transformed me into a spectacular success as a man. Looking back now, it seems as if those days were always filled with sunshine, happiness and shared laughter. The children were thriving, Marylin and I were still very much in love and we had our first family holiday to look forward too.

We stayed at Caister Sands, a self-catering holiday village not far from Great Yarmouth. The weather was gloriously hot the entire fortnight and we had a wonderful time building sand-castles on the beach, teaching the twins to swim, flying kites in the park and even taking our first flight around the coast in an aeroplane. No matter how much time we spent together, Marylin and I never became bored with each other. Although she had a strong character, she never made me feel anything less than a complete man. She was intelligent and interesting, and we always had plenty to talk about. The following year we ventured abroad on a camping holiday in Brittany. Here again, we had such a wonderful time together that we decided to repeat the formula, but to journey further afield each year. We drove to the south of France, then Italy, Switzerland, Austria and even Germany. Though it didn't seem possible, each holiday was better than the one before.

My career at Hoover was going exceedingly well, and after setting up a customer service department I was promoted into marketing, where I discovered that I had a natural flair for solving complicated marketing problems and promoting products. The year we planned our German holiday, I was approached by the troubled Pickles organization which at that time was the sole distributor for ICI gardening and decorative products. The group consisted of three divisions: Pickles, Johnson Wallcoverings, and Saga DIY Retail, of which they appointed me the head. With thirty-two stores ranging in size from 1500 square feet to a virtually unheard-of 82,000, at that time the largest hypermarket in the UK, it was an irresistible challenge.

Since the warehouses and stores were distributed around the country, I spent a lot of time away from home. My secretary, Leslie, often had to accompany me on business trips; it caused much ribbing from the guys in the office but, as I knew our relationship was totally innocent, I just ignored their rather juvenile remarks. When Leslie left she was replaced by a young girl called Sandra Tree. Sandra was quite tall and attractive, with dark, frizzy hair and such a sweet, shy manner that I was amazed when she told me she was in the Territorial Army. I couldn't believe that a girl who seemed so innocent, who blushed as easily as she did, could be interested in something like the TA. Pretty soon it was obvious to everyone that Sandra was completely infatuated with me. She'd often come to our house at weekends and we'd sit in the garden discussing business, or talking about the people we had met on one of our trips away together. It didn't occur to me that there was anything wrong with our friendship, or even that it could be misconstrued by anyone. I was happy with Marylin, and though I was spending more and more time away from home or working late at the office, my reasons for doing so were genuine.

The Saga division of Pickles, which was my main responsibility, was in a bad way financially. Much of it could be put down to the Hoover syndrome of too many people at the top having grown idle and complacent. I was working very hard trying to get to grips with Saga's problems, and it didn't take me long to realize that since so much of the financial bleeding was being caused by security problems at the largest store, in South East England, I should concentrate most of my efforts on reorganizing things there. I spent the next year restructuring the company, selling off 'oddballs' so as to concentrate on more manageable units, establishing a new corporate identity, recruiting additional staff, conceiving more aggressive promotional policies and implementing tight budgetary controls. All this required a great deal of commitment in terms of effort and hours and, though mentally I thrived on the stimulation, physically I began to feel run down.

Once or twice, when Marylin wanted to make love, I'd find myself confronted with the worrying syndrome of 'the spirit being willing but the flesh being weak'. At first I tried telling myself that it was only natural for a man who worked as many hours as I did to feel tired, but when virtually every attempt at intimacy ended in failure I began to worry. For seven wonderful years I'd known nothing but total happiness and contentment, and the prospect of having all that snatched away from me was a real threat to my peace of mind and security. I'd never told Marylin anything about my former problem because it hadn't seemed relevant. But with each repeated failure I began to wish that I had. Instead, I said nothing and, keeping my fears to myself, threw myself more and more into my work. I was caught up in a vicious circle of failure, fear and work, and I didn't know which of the three was aggravating my problem the most.

I started taking paperwork home with me and, as I still insisted on spending lots of time playing with the children before they went to bed, my 'homework' became the perfect excuse for staying up long after Marylin too had retired for the night. It never occurred to me to question what she might be thinking – I was far too wrapped up in the horrors that were once more beginning to invade my own mind. Inexplicable cold shivers of fear would suddenly strike me, though I couldn't work out why. I began to have trouble sleeping, and when I did eventually drop off I'd wake up several times in the night as if I'd had a nightmare whose details I couldn't remember.

When I awoke with a start in the early hours of one morning to find myself shaking and my body soaked in sweat I couldn't deny what was going on: the dreadful spectre that had haunted so much of my life had returned. Sick with fear, I crept out of bed and locked myself in the bathroom. The same question that I'd silently screamed all those years ago was now repeating itself over and over again in my brain. What was wrong with me? Only this time it had a new twist: Why now, when I thought I'd been 'cured'? And then a new thought occurred: Was it possible I could be going insane? Poor Marylin. God knows what she must have thought at that time. Perhaps if I'd been a different kind of man it might have occurred to me that there's only one conclusion a woman will draw when her husband apparently loses all interest in the sexual side of their relationship, and not only spends a great deal of time staying away from home with a good-looking young secretary but even lets her visit him at home. It was only in retrospect that I realized how insensitive I had been, because of course Marylin was perfectly justified in believing that I was having an affair with this girl. In fact her occasional outbursts of intolerance about my relationship with Sandra ought to have alerted me to the situation. My only defence was that I was so wrapped up in my own problems I didn't give a thought to what Marylin might be feeling.

But marriages don't survive long with too many hidden secrets, and eventually Marylin became so upset that she confronted me over my 'affair' with Sandra. I was so aghast that all I could blurt out was: 'My God, Marylin, I can't believe you'd even *think* such a thing!'

'Well, what do you expect?' she said, miserably. 'After all, you spend most of your time with her. You rarely come home before ten o'clock, and calmly tell me you've been working late at the office with her. You stay away with her most of the time. What else am I supposed to think?'

I was so upset that Marylin had been so unhappy for so long and had not said anything to me that I knew there was only one way I could make amends. The moment of truth had finally arrived, and if I wanted to save my marriage I had no choice. In order to reassure Marylin and convince her that I hadn't been having an affair, I must tell her everything. We sat down together and I told her all the things that I should have told her when we first met. Holding nothing back, I explained about the dreams; the problems I had always had with girls; my previous sexual inadequacies; even my fears about not knowing whether there was something seriously wrong with me. And Marylin, bless her, was wonderful. Naturally, her first reaction was relief. I don't think that at that stage either of us had any idea of the enormity of what I was saying, probably because we both assumed that the real problem, whatever it might be, was solvable.

I was so glad that I'd finally been honest with Marylin and got everything off my chest that all I could feel was relief. We both cried as we held on to each other. 'Why didn't you say something sooner?' I asked.

'I was so afraid,' Marylin sobbed. 'I didn't want to lose you. But now I know you weren't having an affair and that you do still love me, everything's going to be all right again.'

If only we had known that nothing was ever really going to be right between us again. Neither of us had any inkling that, far from being the beginning and end of a small difficulty between us, the situation with work and Sandra had merely precipitated the identification of a very serious problem indeed. Moreover, it was one which was to prove totally incurable in any convention-ally acceptable way.

5
SNAKES AND LADDERS

Having discovered, to her immense relief, that I was not involved with another woman, Marylin became more relaxed. I, too, felt as if a great weight had been lifted from my shoulders. Although the problem was still very much in evidence, we both assumed that, given a little time, patience and effort on both sides, it would go away.

Meanwhile, I had responsibilities at work that still required a great deal of my time and effort so I continued to work all hours. One of the first people I came into contact with at Ipswich was Trevor, who owned and edited the *Colchester Leader*, one of the first free newspapers. We hit it off straightaway and quickly became firm friends. Our friendship progressed to the point where Marylin, the children and I would spend weekends with Trevor's family or he would bring his wife and daughter to stay with us.

Having established myself from day one as a hatchet man at the store, naturally I wasn't particularly popular with many of the staff I'd inherited. It wasn't surprising, really, as in order to stop the petty pilfering that had been going on for so long I had to keep a sharp eye on everybody who worked there. Inevitably it meant concentrating most of my time and energy on this one store and soon I was spending the entire week down south and going home to Marylin and the children at weekends.

My plan to turn Saga's fortunes around by disposing of all the oddball stores that were either too large or too small to carry my proposed new standard range was regarded as rather radical. None the less, at first I won the backing of my directors, who agreed to allow me to implement most of my proposals without hindrance. My methods proved a winner. But just how bad the financial position of the group had become was finally brought home to me after I had held a spectacularly successful closing-down sale at Hadleigh, and I received a strange request from the board to send the takings under great security to the group's bank. Out of every £3 I paid into the bank, £2 was immediately taken to pay off the group's enormous debts. The only profitable side of the business – the retail side – was being used to subsidize heavily the unprofitable parts. And, as there wasn't enough money left in the bank to buy the merchandise the stores needed in order to continue trading, we were fast approaching a desperate situation.

Having by this time been given responsibility for all the retail stores, I was aware that extreme measures were called for. I immediately started closing down and cannibalizing some of the smaller stores in order to keep the larger ones operating. But it wasn't enough. Overworked, tired and enormously frustrated, I didn't know which way to turn. I'd purged the group of all its disloyal, lazy staff, and just when I had created a hard-working, loyal and committed workforce it looked as if I was going to have to make them all redundant. What made it even more unfair was that *we* were now the only part of the group making money!

Acutely aware that the company was moving inexorably towards bankruptcy, I discussed my predicament with Trevor. He immediately suggested we consider purchasing the now empty Hadleigh store from Saga and running it ourselves. Trevor was an astute businessman and I knew that his idea had something. We immediately drew up a business plan and approached a merchant bank with our idea. Unfortunately they turned us down, so with great sadness I negotiated the sale of the unit to Tesco's.

By now I was well aware that not even my most drastic measures were going to be enough to keep the company afloat. But then salvation appeared in the form of Gordon Steel, managing director of PGW Retail, a subsidiary of Berger, which was in turn part of the giant West German Hoechst Pharmaceutical Company. Gordon just turned up at the store one day and calmly announced to me that he was thinking about acquiring the entire Pickles organization.

'What's your reaction to that?' he asked in a tone that gave me no indication of what might lie behind the question.

Initially I was very wary, but as we talked I began to realize that, since he was being so forthright and frank with me, the least I could do was return the compliment. Having painted a very bright picture of the group's future should Berger gain control, I knew I had no option other than to support the takeover bid. I duly reported the conversation to my own boss, assuming that everyone at head office would be highly delighted with the prospect of imminent rescue. But within a few days I was left in no doubt that I had seriously miscalculated the situation. Hastily summoned to Yorkshire, I presented myself before the board and was immediately threatened with suspension if I co-operated with Berger or in any way aided their acquisition attempt. Mystified and very angry, I informed the board that as my responsibility was to work for the survival of the company and preserve the job security of my staff, the only course of action open to me was to support Berger's takeover bid.

'Furthermore,' I added angrily, 'if you suspend me I'll report this conversation to the *Daily Telegraph* who, given the investigative series they're currently running on the strategies of this group and the behaviour of certain members of the board, will, I'm sure, greet this information with great interest.'

It was a game of chess – and one that I knew I had a strong chance of winning. With so much at stake, and so many people's jobs depending upon me, I was not about to be intimidated – and it showed.

Berger formalized the takeover offer and Pickles was absorbed into the PGW Group. A few weeks later I presented my proposals for the reshaping of the retail division, based on the relocation and redevelopment of large out-of-town DIY and gardening units, to Gordon Steel and his fellow directors at their Kingston-upon-Thames head office. My proposals were accepted. With Gordon's backing I was appointed divisional controller, allocated a substantial sum of money to put my plans into action and given complete responsibility for everything from buying and merchandizing to marketing and promotions – and a substantial pay rise to boot. With renewed enthusiasm I immediately set about organizing clearance sales, using TV advertizing to promote loss leaders. Following each successful sale the stores were closed down, redesigned and completely restocked with a new mix of merchandise.

I hired Morecambe and Wise to preside over the reopening of the newly refurbished Henlow Camp store, during which Eric Morecambe and I spent a few happy hours reminiscing about my old employer, Councillor Hill, who, amazingly enough, still owned the newsagents where I'd once worked and still supplied Eric with his daily newspapers.

Having outgrown my office, I purchased a Portakabin. Whenever I started work on a new store, my 'office' would simply be loaded on to the back of a lorry and moved to the new site. Most times I'd put in around eighteen or twenty hours a day, without breaking for lunch or even dinner. I lost a substantial amount of weight, my smoking increased to the point where I regularly wheezed my way through forty cigarettes a day, and with all the additional stress and pressure I began once more to look really ill. It was only when I experienced a terrible pain one morning as I pushed Marylin's car down the road to get it started that I realized what I was doing to myself. My heart was pounding fit to burst, my lungs felt like exploding and I was convinced I was about to have a massive heart attack. From that day to this I've never smoked another cigarette.

The moments when I stopped to catch my breath and review my situation, both professionally and personally, were few and far between. But whenever I did have time to think about my life, it struck me as rather ironic that I seemed to be caught up in a real-life game of Snakes and Ladders. On the one hand I was climbing the corporate ladder with great rapidity and my professional star was clearly on the rise, while on the other my personal life was sliding down those snakes with astonishing speed.

It was all very well for me – I could hide behind my work, my constant travelling and the excitement and challenge of solving my corporate dilemmas. But what about Marylin? True, we now had more money to cushion us and there were the children to keep her occupied. But in my heart I knew she needed and deserved far more than that; she needed a husband who came home for supper, not one who, if he turned up at all, crept in at three in the morning and never disturbed her with his touch. But Marylin was marvellous – she remained loving, understanding and incredibly supportive, and I was filled with admiration and guilt. I earned a huge salary and enjoyed a successful career that offered me status, responsibility and a reputation as something of a whizz-kid amongst my colleagues, but as a husband I seemed to be a total failure. I never put it into words, but I couldn't hide it from myself: in every way that really counted, I was letting Marylin down. That's why, though the idea filled me with horror and shame, when Marylin tentatively suggested that we seek medical help I felt I owed it to her to agree.

Together we went to see our GP. This proved a totally useless exercise as, predictably, he put the whole thing down to 'pressure of work'. We went back time and time again until eventually, confounded by something he couldn't understand, he referred me first to a psychologist and then to a psychiatrist. For me the whole thing was humiliating and debasing. I had to endure these people probing into my background and my mind almost as if I was insane. But always at the back of my mind was the thought that what Marylin had been enduring for the past year or two was far, far worse, and because I knew that she had been through more than any woman could – or indeed should have to – put up with I continued with the 'treatment'.

Meanwhile, some of my more imaginative business ideas were beginning to meet with resistance from my superiors. I had negotiated production of a new own-brand range, for which I had designed the containers, and was on the verge of awarding a contract to a manufacturer when I received a directive ordering me not only to give the contract to the Berger division of the group, but also to cease selling competitive brands of paint forthwith. I couldn't understand the company's reasoning. To imagine that stifling the competition would increase our own profitability seemed ludicrous to me. I argued the point, but the board remained adamant. Ignoring my protestations and warnings, the company proceeded to implement a major restructuring of their retailing and marketing strategy which I found wholly unacceptable.

Unfortunately, at one heated moment I had rashly declared that if the new policies were put into effect I would be unable to continue my employment with the group. It was a foolish thing to say because, as is so often the case, the corporate machine rolled on regardless of this (albeit fairly senior) cog in their wheel, and I found myself backed into a corner in which the only exit sign pointed to the door of resignation. Reluctantly and with great regret, I took my leave. Gordon wrote me a really nice letter shortly afterwards, expressing his sorrow at losing 'a valued colleague and business friend' and his sincere appreciation not only for the support I had personally given to him but also for the hard work and effort I had put into my job.

I'd received a rather large *ex gratia* payment from PGW, which not only bought me a little time in which to consider my next professional move but also paid for a 'new' second-hand car for Marylin, who had been very worried and upset at this latest blow. I made one or two applications for jobs but, not wanting to leap too quickly, I took my time evaluating which was the best. Once more I was at home, happy to be spending time with Marylin and the children or pottering about the house and garden doing the hundreds of little jobs that had for so long been ignored.

The psychiatrist whom I had been seeing suggested that I

should try being analysed under hypnosis. It seemed a pretty bizarre idea to me, but having come that far it would have been daft to refuse, particularly as I didn't think they'd have much success hypnotizing me in the first place. When the session was over, he made no mention of what I had said or even what he might have learned, merely suggesting that I take some chromosome tests and come back and see him again. At the time I wasn't aware that Marylin might have been taking anything more than a normal interest in what was going on. She attended most of the sessions with me, except those that involved hypnosis, and when we got home we'd often discuss what had occurred. To be honest, my feeling was that it was all mumbo-jumbo, and nothing so far had caused me to change my long-held belief that psychiatrists are far weirder than any of their patients. However, something that may have been said (or even left unsaid), or some line of reasoning that had been pursued had, as it turned out, given Marylin food for thought. One evening she announced that she was going to the library, and when she returned a few hours later she looked as if she had seen a ghost.

'Keith,' she said a little distractedly, 'let's sit down and talk.'

At first I thought she might want to say something about one of the job offers I'd turned down, or maybe to discuss a minor problem with one of the kids. Though I could see she definitely wasn't her normal, cheerful self, it didn't occur to me that what she was about to reveal would change the course of our lives. I made a pot of tea, carried it through to the lounge and sat down next to Marylin on the settee. There were several minutes of silence as she thoughtfully stirred her tea, put her cup to her lips and took a sip. Then, as if she'd finally reached an important decision, she placed her cup firmly back on its saucer, took my hand between hers and, looking straight into my eyes, uttered the words that, had we only known it then, were to herald the end of our life together.

'Keith, I *know* what's wrong. I know what you *are*.'

Uncomprehending, I could only stare back.

'Keith,' Marylin explained, her voice gentle and patient, 'you're a textbook *transsexual*.'

Her words filled me with horror. 'What on earth are you saying?' I said indignantly. No one had ever uttered the word before, so she couldn't have picked it up from one of the psychologists. Clearly, something that somebody had said had triggered off a new line of reasoning in her head. I could only presume that, having absorbed and recalled everything I'd told her about my past, she had been determined to learn more.

Marylin tried hard to make me understand: 'What you *are* . . . what you *have* is . . . more than the usual amount of feminine traits.'

'I'm not gay!' I hotly denied, upset and annoyed that I was being accused of something, but not quite sure what.

'I don't mean that. I know you're not gay. What it means is that. . . .' It was difficult for Marylin to find the words that would convince me of the truth she now seemed to be so sure of herself. 'Look, think back. Think how you were with the children, the babies, think how you always loved to help me . . . how you've always been able to *understand* me, to *know* intuitively how I feel!'

Not only could I not believe what I was hearing, I was incapable of even beginning to comprehend the enormity of what Marylin was trying to explain. 'Well, yes, I've always cooked a lot, but lots of men do.'

'Look, you've fathered children, so there can't be anything *physically* wrong with you . . . but, inside you. . . .'

I must have looked in total shock and Marylin, unable to get through to me, was growing more upset and frustrated with each attempt. 'Remember how *naturally* you helped me with the twins when they were born? How *easily* you adapted to being their 'mother' when I had a threatened miscarriage?'

'But lots of other men have done all those things,' I protested.

Marylin took a deep breath. Then, very quietly she said: 'Okay, then think about your *dreams*, for God's sake!'

I'd thought about those dreams – God knows I'd hardly ever *stopped* thinking about those damned dreams – but somehow I couldn't relate them to what Marylin was telling me now. If you add two and two together, you expect four, but what I'd just been told didn't add up at all. If Marylin had said to me, 'You've got a loose wire, a loose connection in your brain', I could have lived with that, but what she was telling me was something far, far worse. The word had been spoken, and now that whatever it was had been given a name, it seemed more monstrously real. If someone says to you, 'You've got a problem with your red blood cells – they're not right,' you might be concerned. But if they tell you, 'You've got leukaemia,' well, once you've been given the name, then it exists. Now you can go and look up all the statistics about leukaemia, and you might find, for example, that 54 per cent of cancer sufferers die. Then you can't help but become really terrified.

We both began to weep, me trying hard to cling on to my sanity in the awful light of what I had just heard but couldn't quite believe, and Marylin trying to cling on to me amidst the dreadful certainty of what she now knew to be true. How terrible it must have been for Marylin. To discover that the man you've loved and lived with for many years, the man who's fathered your children, is emotionally and mentally a woman is bad enough – but to have to be the one to convince that man of the truth about himself. How did she find the strength to do it? I don't know how long we sat there, holding on to each other, neither of us wanting to believe. I was totally numb, paralysed with the shock of it all.

Eventually, Marylin said, 'Come upstairs with me. There's something I'd like to do.'

Meekly, I followed her. When we got to the bedroom Marylin sat me down on the bed, like a child without a will of its own, and proceeded to pull clothes out of her wardrobe.

'Here, put this on,' she said.

I could only stare in amazement as Marylin handed me one of her dresses.

'Wh . . . what are you doing?' I asked.

'Just do it, Keith. Put my dress on. Let me make up your face. I just want to see, *to know*, how you feel.'

At five feet seven or thereabouts Marylin was fairly tall for a woman, though still several inches shorter than me. She was also a lot slighter in build. But I did what she wanted – I struggled into her dress and sat there while she applied make-up to my face.

When she had finished, Marylin whispered, 'Now, tell me how you feel.'

'I feel – well, normal, I guess,' I replied.

'What!' Marylin's voice was shrill with nervous tension.

'What I mean is, I feel how I normally feel, maybe even a bit stupid – that's all.'

I think what Marylin had been trying to do was to ascertain whether I felt different in any way, or maybe even sexually turned on; to discover whether I might have transvestite tendencies. But I didn't. I felt slightly silly, but mostly just peaceful. I didn't want to rush out and display myself to the world. I didn't suddenly want to drag her off to bed and ravish her. Apart from the strangeness of wearing women's clothing for the first time since I was a child, I didn't really feel any different at all.

That night we held each other close in bed, neither of us saying much – what was there to say? – both of us unable to sleep. Marylin must have been distraught, but all her concern was for me. The following day we tried to carry on as normal. Neither of us mentioned Marylin's revelation of the previous evening, probably because neither of us could think what to do next. And, as the old saying goes, 'When in doubt, do nowt.'

The one thing I did do, though, was immediately cancel all my appointments with the psychiatrist. I'd listened to something I didn't want to hear, and I had no intention of allowing things to go any further than that. If there truly was something wrong with me, I'd sort it out on my own – I didn't need anyone else interfering in my life. And so I buried the knowledge that I didn't want to believe. Not being able to face the enormity of it, I simply blocked it out of my consciousness and thus out of my life.

On a recent family holiday in Wales I'd seen a huge building standing empty in large grounds. When I made enquiries locally I learned that it had been a hotel before being converted into a mental hospital. I'd been mulling over the germ of an idea to open up a residential activity centre. Trevor and I had taken our defeat over the Hadleigh store fairly bitterly, and we were both determined to find a business that we could develop together. Now I decided to throw all my energies into pursuing this particular project, because work was the only thing I knew that could occupy every corner of my mind.

I arranged for Trevor to come and stay at our house the night before we made the journey to Wales. We set off with high hopes, but after viewing the interior of the building, whose badly dilapidated state seemed to echo the neglect of all those sad patients who had once called it home, we had to acknowledge defeat. The cost of converting it into anything even approaching a habitable state was far beyond our means.

Once we'd got over our disappointment we decided that, rather than waste the entire journey, we might as well tour the countryside and see if anything else caught our eye. Something did. But it wasn't a building – it was a railway! The Bala Lake Railway principals were experiencing severe difficulties in financing the necessary restoration work, we learned, and therefore might welcome a takeover bid. Alas, this scheme too was doomed to failure; there were far too many shareholders to convince, and every single one was not only a friend or relative of one of the principals, but also a dedicated enthusiast. .

In a sombre mood, Trevor and I set off home. Now that I no

longer had an exciting new project to occupy my mind, thoughts of my personal predicament came flooding back and during the journey I found myself confessing all the harrowing details of my past – and particularly my present – problems to Trevor, who to his credit listened patiently throughout. What I hadn't yet told him was that some weeks before I had had what I thought was a brilliant idea. When I'd first mentioned it to Marylin she had (quite rightly, I acknowledged much later) been absolutely appalled. But so convinced had I been that my idea provided the perfect solution to many of our problems that I'd persisted in my attempts to make her first understand, and then agree to, my crazy plan.

That plan was that Marylin should take a lover – not just *any* lover, but one whom we both knew and trusted. After all, I had reasoned, if I was incapable of being a complete husband to Marylin, how long would it be before she might turn her eyes elsewhere? And if she should take a lover, what would that do to our marriage? Wouldn't it make better sense – and be far safer and more controllable – this way?

At first horrified and outraged, Marylin had refused to listen. But I hadn't let the matter drop. I had since brought it up time and time again. I'd used every persuasive argument I could think of in an attempt to convince her of the sense of my plan. Eventually, worn down by a series of lengthy, 'logical' arguments backed up by continual pleading, she had reluctantly given in. Now all that was left was for me to persuade Trevor to agree.

It seemed so simple at the time; so logical and neat and sensible. In reality it proved to be the worst decision of my life. Moreover, it was one that I would always bitterly regret. Trevor knew nothing of my mental ramblings as he sat beside me in the car, silently digesting what he had just heard. He asked me several questions to clarify certain things in his mind and then, incredulously, he said: 'I had no idea! Why didn't you tell me all this sooner?'

After giving him the only explanation I could – that I myself hadn't fully understood what was wrong with me – I hesitantly put forward the crazy plan I had been formulating. 'The thing is, Trevor, though I can satisfy Marylin with oral sex, how long can I expect her to remain content with that? Surely it would be far kinder, and fairer, if I were to find a way of ensuring that Marylin could enjoy a physical relationship outside. of our marriage?'

Never one to beat about the bush, Trevor didn't disappoint me now. 'So you're inviting me to go to bed with your wife, right?'

Put like that, it sounded so premeditated and cold.

'Don't you see, Trevor? You'd be perfect! You both know each other well. You like each other a lot. Neither of you is likely to become deeply involved and, besides, the distance alone means it need never be more than a very occasional event.'

Trevor didn't respond and, thinking it was better to let him mull the idea over in his mind, I let the matter drop. When we arrived home, I had a few words with Marylin in private. She was aghast but, after I had persuaded her once again that it really would be the best thing to do, she reluctantly seemed to accept the idea. The children were in bed when the three of us ate dinner together. As soon as I'd washed up, I left Marylin and Trevor alone together and went up to bed. Marylin joined me at seven the following morning, just before the children woke up.

I don't think I can ever describe adequately the emotions this experience aroused in me. Although I honestly believe that all I wanted was what was best for Marylin and for our marriage, I had no idea how difficult I would find it coming to terms with the result. It's all very well to conceive a plan that seems right logically, but logic doesn't ever make any allowances for emotion, and emotionally I just couldn't handle it. For the first time in my life I became jealous, irrational and highly possessive. And while Marylin's liaison with Trevor was sporadic, to say the least, each time they slept together it only served to increase my mental pressure rather than to alleviate it. It's occurred to me since that Marylin might, in retrospect, feel that my own guilt was pushing me to create situations in which she would inevitably feel guilty, too. I've thought long and hard about my own motives, but I honestly don't feel that was so.

As it had never been a real love affair, it wasn't long before the relationship (if that's what it can be called) between Marylin and Trevor began to drift apart. Trevor was experiencing his own problems at home, which were totally separate from Marylin, and not long afterwards his marriage broke up. When he met another lovely young woman, he rightly decided to stop sleeping with Marylin. It was a decision which I believe Marylin was happy to concur with.

Somehow, Marylin and I managed to survive the next few years. A new job in the North of England as sales and marketing director with the Hestair Group, one of the leading contractors in the field of educational supplies, did much to distract both our minds from the problems neither of us wanted to face. Once again I was fired into action by this new career challenge and, although we were reluctant to move so far away, it had to be done. We put our house on the market, sold it the same day and moved in with my parents, who fortunately had two spare bedrooms, until we could find something suitable near my new job. I embarked on a weekly cycle of commuting between Manchester, where I worked in the week, and Harpenden, where I spent the weekends.

Six months were to pass before we found the perfect home in Darwen, Lancashire – a rambling, six-bedroomed house called Wynthorpe. It was love at first sight. We couldn't get over the fact that, in addition to having a one-and-a-half-acre garden, we had a large lounge and dining room, a massive kitchen, a utility room and our very own wine cellar. However, not even the luxury of our new life could stop Marylin from feeling homesick, and she never really settled in the North.

I threw myself into my new job with the same vigour I always did, and it didn't take me long to find out that the challenge I'd taken up was even greater than I had anticipated. I was horrified to learn that we were committed to an average of twenty-seven educational exhibitions each year, with all the attendant costs of such exercises. What nobody had ever set out to analyse was just how much commercial sense these exhibitions made. So I decided to attend one of them myself. As I suspected, most were just an excuse for married men to stay away from home and play around like schoolboys.

One of my first tasks was to sort out the huge, full-colour catalogue which was sent to every school in the country. Once again I was appalled, because even the basic principles of marketing were being ignored. Instead of applying a sensible pricing structure that reflected the uniqueness of certain lines as most companies do, Hestair operated a set formula of marking up by a fixed percentage on cost regardless. The result was that some items would be priced at £1.01 when, of course, they should have been rounded down to 99 pence while others should have been priced a great deal higher simply because they were unobtainable elsewhere. I was going to have to scrap the new catalogue, which had only just been printed, arrange for every single product to be re-photographed and then have the whole thing rewritten. In addition to that, the entire pricing structure required radical reformulation in order to make commercial sense. It was a wonder how a company operating with so many handicaps could have survived.

I drew up a master plan and then implemented the most radical changes the company had ever seen. I scrapped the majority of venues on our exhibition schedule, retaining just six which I thought might possibly produce something worthwhile. I replaced every technical expert the company employed with a sales or marketing professional, and went out to competitive tendering for photography, typesetting and print on the new catalogue. The result was a bigger, better catalogue at a reduced cost per page. I then developed computer programs capable of analysing order input, margin price and relative earnings per catalogue page. I also cancelled the science equipment catalogue that had only achieved sales of £20,000 on a stockholding five times that figure before travelling to Czechoslovakia to negotiate a deal that reduced the product range by 90 per cent. Having virtually worked round the clock for weeks, during which time I had sweated blood and tears on proposals which would either consolidate my position within the company or lead to disaster, all I could do now was mail out the catalogue to every school in the country and then sit back and wait for the verdict.

Vindication was mine! Turnover immediately leaped by 40 per cent, with an accompanying 5 per cent rise in gross margins. Better still, I was given the immediate go-ahead to exploit both the contract and export sides of the business. Soon, contract after contract was falling into our eager hands. From being a fifth-rate regional supplier, within five years we had moved to take over the market leader slot.

I might have been instrumental in the company's amazing turnaround, but I knew that staying ahead of the game required even more work. So I formulated an idea for a competition to encourage people in the educational sector to submit their own ideas for a new product or teaching aid. We developed my idea in conjunction with the *Times Educational Supplement* and launched the 'Brainwave Awards', which proved to be so successful that they soon became an annual event.

Hot on the heels of that success, I was approached by an eccentric, likeable Welshman called Rupert Oliver. Rupert's concept, so simple and yet so brilliant, has now become known as a 'totally soft play environment' (TSPE) for blind and handicapped children. It involved first padding the walls and floor of a room with a foam material covered in tough, washable

PVC; this room would then be filled with enormous shapes such as giant balls, circles, mountains, slides and so on, all constructed from the same soft protective materials. We placed the first installation at the Royal School for the Blind in Edinburgh, and I went along to witness at first hand how the children would cope with this unique equipment. The memory of that day will stay with me for as long as I live, and as I flew home that evening I felt immensely humbled at what I had experienced with those wonderful children who lived in a world of darkness and had to rely totally on their hands to 'see'.

Over the next seven years, success followed success as I began to spend more time travelling abroad to straighten out the export side of Hestair's business. I'd climbed a long way up the corporate ladder, and though it was tough getting to the top, the ambitious streak I discovered within me meant that I revelled in every tiring, hard-working minute of my climb. Professionally, it seemed I could now do no wrong. But in my personal life things were going from bad to worse, and my relationship with Marylin was sliding downhill fast.

6
ROCK BOTTOM

With Trevor now safely ensconced in a new relationship – but still very much a good friend to both Marylin and myself – Marylin still took the occasional lover, but there was no one serious. Despite the fact that she obviously needed a form of love and comfort that I was unable to give her, I think, in fact, these brief flings brought her little satisfaction. Although it had been me who had pushed Marylin down that rocky path, I still hadn't found a way to reconcile my intense feelings of jealousy and rejection whenever I knew there was someone else on the scene.

We had a large house that was luxurious by most people's standards, three wonderful children who were intelligent, healthy and carefree, and an enviable lifestyle. Though Marylin wasn't particularly happy about our move north, and the children found it a bit of a culture shock, the fact that we were altogether again as a family more than compensated for the things she missed about living in the south. Rebecca quickly made friends with a little girl who lived nearby and Stephen and Andrew, who were in the last year of primary school, soon settled in at the Ashleigh Junior School. I had a career that gave me immense satisfaction and pride, and though Marylin still missed her family in the south she found some consolation in the part-time job she had found working with a local Tory Party agent. Through being united in our efforts not to allow the problems within our own relationship to affect the children, we had learned to evolve our own methods for making our life together reasonably tolerable. Taking all these factors into account, it's not surprising that outsiders assumed we were the ideal family. We socialized a fair bit – I belonged to the local Round Table, and there was always a fund-raising soirée to attend at the local Tory Party's HQ. It was during the course of a social evening organized by the Round Table that Marylin first got to know David.

David was a very successful local businessman who ran his own company supplying men and equipment under contract to local power stations and offshore oil installations. I never particularly liked him, probably because he seemed to have every-thing I lacked: he was extrovert, popular, successful and appeared to have both unlimited wealth and unlimited free time. Of course, David had other things too, like a wife and three children, but that didn't seem to be a deterrent, and before too long I became aware that what I had assumed to be just another of Marylin's casual liaisons was fast developing into a full-blown affair. To add insult to injury, when I confronted Marylin with my jealous accusations I learned that David had something else that I didn't – he was incredibly good in bed!

Something was happening, and this time it was beyond the control of either of us. Soon, discretion was abandoned in the face of desire and Marylin and David's affair became common knowledge. They'd meet at lunchtime in a local pub and then spend the afternoon in a motel at Bolton. I asked Marylin to stop seeing him, but, too infatuated to care about what people thought, she refused. I blamed myself for having pushed her into a situation in which sooner or later she was bound to meet somebody special, but knowing it was my own fault didn't make the pain any less real or easier to deal with.

Things began to get out of hand. David's wife knew, the whole village knew and pretty soon it became obvious that our children knew too. This was brought home to me when I discovered that Stephen, Andrew and Becky had written a note begging David to 'please leave our mummy alone' and posted it through his letter box. It was that incident, more than anything else, that demonstrated to me the price that my family were being forced to pay, and I wept for the pain and suffering I had unwittingly inflicted upon the wife and children I loved so much.

By day I continued to do my job to the best of my abilities, while at night I stayed awake, worrying and weeping about the new dilemma we all faced. Slowly, my mind began to buckle. The enormous pressure of years of pent-up strain began to show and I didn't know which way to turn.

Marylin became even bolder about her relationship with David, seeing him at night and occasionally spending whole weekends away with him, too. I couldn't cope and started to behave irrationally, often walking the streets at four in the morning looking for her so that I could beg her to come home. Then one night I snapped, and hit her around the face. No man should ever strike a woman, no matter how much he is pro-voked. My shame and desolation couldn't have been greater.

Now that I was behaving so out of character, the children couldn't help but be aware of what was going on.

In desperation I went to see my GP who, having access to my file and therefore the psychiatrist's notes, just looked at me with great sympathy and told me gently that in his considered opinion there was only one way out – I must become a woman. Still, I refused to believe him. There *must* be something that could be done, some way out of this mess. I was frantic, unable to accept that this was the end of the road for my marriage, but too weak to decide what else we could do. Frightened, lost and helpless, like a man in the grip of a witch doctor's spell, I retreated to my bed where I stayed for eight weeks. I lay there like a zombie, wanting only to die. The awful dream that had for so long tormented my nights now spilled over to haunt my days as well. What made it even more unbearable was that I knew Marylin was also going through a private hell of her own. I had been the one to wear her resistance down, to convince her that the only sensible thing to do was for her to have relationships outside our marriage, and now that she was involved with someone who meant something special to her I was acting like a jealous lunatic.

Meanwhile, my work was suffering. Although I dragged myself out of bed to go on a Far Eastern trip that had been planned months before, once I was out there I became so ill that the company had to fly me straight back home. I returned in an even worse state than when I'd left. Worse still, I learned that Marylin had apparently left the children with friends while she had spent a few days down south with David during my absence. I was beginning to go insane. Though my memory of those days is still far from clear, it seems that on one particular occasion I even flew out of my bed and dashed around the house screaming as I held my head in my hands. All poor Marylin could do was sit on the stairs and sob her heart out. I can't begin to imagine what her life must have been like during those months. I only know that I put her through hell – and that's something I don't think I'll ever forgive myself for. Neither of us knew what to do and both of us were beyond sorting ourselves out, let alone helping each other.

The crisis came one night after yet another harrowing scene in which I'd begged Marylin to stay home that evening. Appalled with myself for having collapsed at her feet, a pathetically sobbing, pleading wreck who had abandoned all pretence of self-respect, I finally admitted to myself that things had gone too far; we couldn't go on destroying each other any more. We were both desolate and, in my case at least, that misery was compounded by the knowledge that there was only one person who was truly to blame. That night I reached a decision. My doctor was wrong when he said there was only *one* way out of my present predicament. For, with nothing now left to live for, there was another way out; as I had been the cause of all our problems, so I was the only one who could solve them. Therefore the simplest, the kindest and the fairest thing I could do would be to put an end to all our suffering.

My decision made, I felt nothing but a strange sense of peace flowing through me. The desperation, the panic, the trauma would soon be a thing of the past. I checked to make sure the children were still asleep, then I sat down and wrote a note to Marylin explaining my thoughts and feelings, asking for her forgiveness for all that I had put her through and reassuring her that in no way was she to blame. To be as I was was not anybody's fault. Knowing that people have a tendency to blame themselves when things go wrong, I wanted only to reassure Marylin now. It wasn't her fault, it wasn't my parents' fault, it wasn't even God's fault – it was just the way things were.

I was counting out the tablets into my palm, preparing to swallow them one by one, when the telephone rang. I hesitated, not knowing whether I should answer or just let it ring. Fate dictated. It was Trevor. Had he had some kind of premonition? Or was it sheer coincidence? Trevor and I had grown so close over the years, it was useless my trying to deny anything was wrong when he could tell just from the sound of my voice.

'Keith, whatever you're thinking about or planning, don't do it – it's not worth it,' Trevor insisted. 'Promise me, Keith, that you won't do whatever is in your mind?'

Trevor stayed on the phone for what seemed like hours as he talked to me, saying the same thing over and over again. Eventually he made me give him my word that I wouldn't commit suicide, but just to make sure he insisted that I ring him again in half an hour. 'If I don't get your call, I'll phone your local police station immediately and I'm going to get straight into my car and drive up there,' he warned.

I knew Trevor would do just as he had threatened, so I returned his call not once but many times, because on each occasion he extracted yet another promise that I'd call him again at the end of the next half-hour. Tired beyond belief, I abandoned all thought of suicide and eventually managed to convince Trevor that my darkest moment had passed. I'm sure we were both relieved to fall into our beds.

I don't know what time Marylin came home, but when I awoke she had left for work. Feeling like hell, I stumbled into the bathroom and saw my reflection staring back at me in the mirror. One glance was enough to convince me that I looked like hell, too. You've got to *do* something, I told myself. Make a decision. Either kill yourself or have medical treatment, because you certainly can't go on living like this. Either way I'd lose my beloved Marylin and our three children, and faced with *that*, surely suicide must be the best way out?

Once again I toyed with the idea. How would my parents cope with the news that they had a son who might soon become their daughter? How would my wife come to terms with the fact that her husband was going to become a woman himself? And, worst of all, what psychological damage might it do to my children if they discovered that their father could soon be their second mother? No truly sane individual could possibly make the people he loves go through that. And if I decided to live and go through with the change, what would my life be like?

Over the years, both Marylin and I had learned a little more about the word 'transsexual'. We both knew that the only course of action involved three years of hormone treatment before painful and dangerous surgery. Gender reassignment, the technical term for the process of changing sex, seemed to me to be a long, hard, unrewarding road that would cost me absolutely everything I had achieved and everything I held dear. But more than that, I couldn't conceive that there could be any worthwhile kind of life beyond it.

For hours I wrestled with my problem, uncertain what to do for the best. On the one hand, part of me wanted to die right then; on the other, something kept whispering in my mind that if it hadn't been for Trevor, I wouldn't be alive now. Could that mean that my moment of truth had come and gone? My mind had been made up, but something about Trevor's uncanny sense of timing seemed to me to be a sign. And then I knew that my very last option had gone. I had to face it – there *was* only one way out, now. I would go through with it. I'd finally do what I had not had the courage even to think about for the past seven years. I would become a woman.

When Marylin came home from work we had the most sensible – and certainly the calmest – conversation we had had in a long time as I outlined what I had decided. Having made up my mind, I felt incredibly calm. All the anger, the trauma, the pain and the fear had gone, and for the first time in several years I felt at peace.

Having asked Marylin to think carefully about what I had chosen to do, she came back with the suggestion that I wait for two months. I remember it ws just before Christmas, and though we both had a great deal on our minds, it was probably one of the nicest Christmases we'd had in many years. When the two months were up, Marylin asked for more time. I didn't mind, I knew what *I* had to do – all I needed now was Marylin's support.

A month later Marylin gave me her answer: 'I've thought long and hard about this, Keith, and if this is the only way in which you can live, then it must be the right thing to do.'

I was so overcome with emotion that at first, I found it hard to speak. Then I said, 'Do you think you could keep supper warm for a while? I want to go out.'

'You're not planning to do anything silly, are you?' she asked anxiously.

'Of course not,' I replied. And with that I backed the car out of the drive, went straight to the newsagent's for a copy of the *Manchester Evening News* and drove up on to the moors, where I sat for a while scanning the accommodation ads.

I made a phone call, arranged to view a flat the very next day and then went home to Marylin. The next day I paid six months' advance rent on my new home.

Marylin and I had discussed what we would tell the children and the only plausible explanation we had been able to come up with was to say that I had an illness for which the only cure was intensive hormone treatment. That treatment, we said, would result in my becoming a woman. Though Stephen and Andrew were thirteen, and Rebecca even younger, I don't think they were old enough or mature enough to absorb fully what we were saying. None of them said a word – they merely clung to me and cried.

There was a lump in my throat as I looked at Marylin's face. Leaving her was the hardest thing I've ever had to do, but by now we were both resigned to the fact that the die had finally been cast in a bizarre game that had begun long before we had even met.

As I settled into my new flat in Walsden, not even the lack of creature comforts such as heating, gas or lighting, which had not yet been connected, could detract from the incredible sense of relief at having finally made such a momentous move. For seven long, traumatic years I had refused to acknowledge the truth about myself. My denial had caused me to inflict more pain on Marylin than anyone has the right to inflict on someone they love, and I felt bitterly ashamed of my selfishness. I knew, too, that I was the only person who would benefit from what I was about to do. For those whom I loved, there could only be more suffering.

Two weeks later I signed on with a new doctor in Todmorden, and though he was undoubtedly nonplussed to be confronted by this near six-foot specimen of manhood announcing that he wanted to become a woman, I have to say he rose remarkably to the occasion. Dr Ryland listened patiently, oblivious to the queue that was building up in his waiting room and then, after admitting that he knew nothing whatsoever about transsexuals, assured me that he would make it his business to gather all the information he could before my next visit. True to his word, he contacted my old GP in Darwen and then made a special trip to Wythenshawe Hospital to consult a specialist psychologist who treated people like me.

Like so many people who are continually confronted with the bleakest aspects of life, Dr Ryland had long since learnt the value of humour to relieve the seriousness of living, and under his wonderful care I soon found my sense of humour returning. Thus it wasn't long before my regular trips to his surgery became one of the brighter points of my week.

'I'm going to refer you to a specialist by the name of Dr Hoare,' he informed me during one visit. 'He also happens to treat alcoholics, so don't be alarmed if when you go to see him at Wythenshawe his reception area is full of men clutching brown paper bags.'

'Crikey!' I said, 'I've just about got used to the idea of being a TS. Do you think I can cope with being regarded as an alcoholic, too?'

We got on so well that we were even able to make a joke about the hormone treatment he began to give me. 'I'm going to put you on a drug called Androcur and another called Premarin, which is a synthetic form of oestrogen. Its name is derived from the way in which it's produced – it comes from *pregnant mares' urine.*'

'Which gives a whole new meaning to the phrase "taking the piss",' I laughed.

Dr Ryland told me that the Androcur was designed to inhibit

the production of male hormones, while the Premarin would at the same time flood my body with female hormones. Within six months the Androcur should ensure virtual chemical castration. At the same time I would also be given an appointment to see Dr Russell Reid, the famous consultant Psychiatrist at Charing Cross Hospital's Gender Reassignment Clinic, who would monitor my progress at three-monthly intervals.

There was one awkward moment when I took my prescription to the local chemist. When I handed it over, the female pharmacist gave me a very odd look before taking me aside to whisper: 'There must be some mistake. These are *female* hormones your doctor's prescribed!'

'I know,' I whispered back. 'I'm a woman in disguise.'

'Oh!' was all she could say. But her face was a picture!

Highly embarrassed, I hung around, desperately trying to look nonchalant as she went off to make up the prescription. Despite feeling uncomfortable, I was acutely aware that this was just the beginning, and if I couldn't put up with a little bit of embarrassment then I might as well give up now.

As soon as I got home, I shook the pills out on to the table and just sat looking at them. *This is it,* I told myself nervously. *Once you've swallowed these, the decision will be irrevocable.* With shaking hands I filled a glass with water, put the pills in my mouth and gulped them down – and the strange thing was that the moment I'd swallowed them an overwhelming sense of contentment swept through me. Even now, when I think back on that moment, I experience the same kind of thrill. It was the moment I truly knew I had made the right decision.

Over the next few months I watched spellbound as the gradual feminization of my body took place. Slowly, I developed breasts and hips and my waistline began to narrow. My skin became softer and smoother as the rate of hair and beard growth slowed down. I knew that by the time I started my three-monthly meetings at Charing Cross with Dr Reid, who would be counselling me and vetting my progress, I would have to prove beyond a shadow of a doubt that I could cope with travelling and staying in London looking, to all intents and purposes, just like a woman. Back at work, however, where no one had the slightest idea of the treatment I was undergoing, it soon became necessary for me to keep my suit jacket on always and to wear larger shirts in order to conceal my by now sizeable breasts.

As I was earning around £26,000 a year, which was a

stupendous salary in the early eighties, I was able to handle all my financial commitments to Marylin and the children quite comfortably. I still saw the family fairly often. We'd even have dinner together at times, and though we were getting on better than we had done in years, I think she found coming to terms with the changes in me difficult to handle – as I'm sure anyone would. Our parents were devastated by the news of our separation, as indeed were most people who knew us. Marylin and I had made a pact not to discuss my impending 'change' with anybody else until it was absolutely necessary and, ignorant of the true reason for our divorce, my parents naturally sided with me while Marylin's mother sided with her.

Despite the hormones, my facial hair growth was not diminishing as fast as it should have done, so I made an appointment with a lovely motherly woman called Betty who, I was told, would use electrolysis to deal with the problem. Three times a week, from seven-thirty till ten-thirty in the morning, I'd steel myself to visit Betty and undergo the most painful form of treatment I have ever had in my entire life. When it comes to pain, I have a very low tolerance level. Added to that, I have an absolute horror of needles, so you can imagine what an ordeal electrolysis was for me. People often ask me questions about the actual operation and how painful it was, but believe me, I'd rather go through the operation twice over than have to endure the agony of electrolysis again. To my mind, if anything is going to put a man off going through with gender reassignment, it's electrolysis. My face began to look sore and red, and though at work I was able to pass this off as a reaction to shaving, the first time Marylin noticed she knew immediately what it meant. I think that was possibly the first time that what I was about to do really hit her. Soon afterwards, she announced that she was going to move down south to live with her mother.

I was shattered. It hadn't occurred to me that she might move away, though of course it was a logical and reasonable thing for her to consider. All I could think of was that it might be ages before I'd see her or the children again. I travelled down south to see Marylin and the children settle in. The private education they had received up until now didn't necessarily qualify the children for admission to the grammar schools we wanted them to attend. However, I was able to use my position at Hestair to make an appointment with the heads of their prospective schools and, much to our relief, the children were accepted. That night we all went out for a meal to celebrate. The following day I drove back north on my own, feeling dejected and low.

A few months later, I was approached by a headhunter to discuss a potential new job. Fison's, a well-known company that sold horticultural and DIY products, would like to meet me with a view to inviting me to work my magic on their subsidiary company, Griffin and George, who, like Hestair, were involved in the educational supplies market. I duly had my meeting with the Fison's board and was made an offer which, while it certainly exceeded the package I had with Hestair, wasn't significant enough on its own to tempt me to leave. What *was* tempting was the prospect of getting my teeth into another challenge.

Quite coincidentally, at the same time that I was considering this offer Stuart, my chairman and managing director, called me into his office. 'As you're well aware, Keith,' he said, 'our turnover is now in excess of £20 million, and as we're considering making a sizeable investment in expansion through acquisition I believe it's time we separated the role of chairman and MD.'

I waited patiently for Stuart to unfold his plans.

'I'd like you to become our new MD.'

I was so surprised I didn't know what to say. Rapidly evaluating my position, I spent the next few moments concentrating my thoughts. Here I was, with an enviable and successful track record, being confronted with the opportunity to fulfil all my career ambitions by not one but two large, well-respected companies. And yet, after eighteen months of hormone treatment, I knew that it would only be another year or so before I would change my sex. I had planned to stay with Hestair in my present position for the next year or eighteen months, and then quietly leave before the operation. Afterwards, I had thought I might open a restaurant or hotel somewhere.

'I'm sorry, Stuart. I'm afraid I'm going to have to turn the offer down,' I calmly said.

Now it was Stuart's turn to be surprised. For several moments neither of us spoke as he sat there digesting my statement. Then he rose from his chair and began to pace around his office. 'You can't mean that, Keith, surely? I mean, if it's a question of money . . . .'

It wasn't the money. It wasn't even the offer from Fison's. But would Stuart believe or accept that? And if he didn't accept that, what explanation would satisfy him? My mind raced as I tried to think up a plausible reason for refusing what we both knew was a splendid opportunity. But I couldn't think of even one. In the end, knowing that I had to give a reason, I opted to tell the truth.

'If you've got an hour to spare, Stuart, I think you'd better sit down and hear what I have to say.' Fully anticipating that I would tell him I was resigning to take up a better job, Stuart sat down to hear me out. An hour later, having sat through my entire story without uttering a single word or trying to interrupt once, he was at a complete loss for words. Then, shaking his head in amazement, the only words he could find were: 'Well, in my long career I thought I'd come across every conceivable personnel problem in the book, but I have to say this one's a new one on me.' Then, 'My first reaction is to tell you that I don't want to lose you. However, I think I need some time to let this sink in. Perhaps it would be a good idea if we discussed this over dinner somewhere privately tomorrow night.'

The next night we went to a small restaurant in Rochdale where Stuart informed me that, having given the matter much thought, he felt fairly certain that the staff, our suppliers and the board had enough respect for my abilities to accept my situation and offer me their wholehearted support. 'After all,' he concluded, 'it's only your body that's changing, not your brain.'

On hearing this wonderful news, I rapidly discarded my previous plans and gratefully and speedily accepted his offer to stay on in my present position as marketing director.

With my future now secure, I embarked on the next step of learning how to be a woman. I was introduced to Sandra, a young beautician who would teach me how to put on make-up, to walk, stand and comport myself as a woman, and who would accompany me on shopping trips for all the accessories I'd need for my new life. Over the next year Sandra proved to be a remarkable friend, always cheerful, supportive and endlessly patient as she demonstrated over and over again the correct way to apply cosmetics or explain why a certain outfit would do nothing for me at all. And a true friend she has remained ever since.

I couldn't conceive how I might look as a woman, but I was determined that, no matter how much work and practice it took, I wasn't going to look like a man in drag – particularly as Dr Ryland had told me that the next time I visited his surgery I was to come dressed in women's clothes. Every detail of that day, from the moment I walked out of my front door to the moment I returned, is etched on my memory in vivid detail.

My appointment was at five in the afternoon and I allowed myself four hours to get ready. I left work at lunchtime and rushed home to prepare myself. I was sweating so much through fear and nervousness that I was terrified my make-up would run. As I drove into Todmorden, I was shaking from head to foot. The reception area was laid out with chairs all facing the front, which meant that only the people sitting next to me would be able to get a good look. The problem was, we were called four at a time to go along a corridor and sit on the four chairs that were lined up against the wall outside the doctor's surgery door. By the time my name was called I was panicking so much that I was sopping wet with sweat, and as I clattered along in my unfamiliar heeled shoes I was convinced that everyone in the reception area was laughing behind my back. When I finally got into Dr Ryland's office I could only collapse weakly into a chair.

'How do you feel?' he asked sympathetically.

'Exhausted ... a bleeding nervous wreck! It's taken so much out of me I feel terrible,' was all I could say.

Dr Ryland smiled. 'Actually, you look quite good.'

The moment I got home I poured myself a large vodka and tonic to calm my shattered nerves. If a brief visit to my own doctor could have this effect on me, how on earth would I cope with having to travel all the way to London as a woman to see Dr Reid? Thinking about *that* daunting prospect reminded me that it was now imperative for me to decide on my new feminine name. I'd been advised to choose a three-syllable christian name but no more than a two-syllable surname because, I was told, if I chose a short christian name people would always say 'Pardon?'

I spent hours writing down three-syllable female names like Margaret, Isabel and Antoinette and then coming up with another girl's christian name to tack on the end. As I'd been warned about the danger of having three initials that spelled something embarrassing when put together, I'd sat for hours toying with various name combinations to ensure that I didn't end up with a name like Tina Isabel Turner which might inadvertently cause a problem. I didn't have a clue what I wanted to be called; I just knew that I wanted to incorporate something that reminded me of the children. So I put Stephen and Andrew together and came up with Stephanie Anne.

When it came to a suitable surname I was stumped. It was only when I received a call from the hospital asking which name my appointment should be made in that the solution presented itself to me. As I cast my eyes frantically around my flat, looking

Above: Mum, Dad, me and my sister Pearl

Right: The young Casanova

Marrying Marylin: one of the happiest days of my life

ur first home, a semi-detached house in Harpenden

1968, the twins, Stephen and Andrew are born

As sales and marketing director of Hestair, I launched the national schools chess championships

Soon after the divorce, I am lucky enough still to have free access to the twins and Rebecca

for inspiration, my gaze fell upon my chequebook on the table. It bore the legend 'Lloyds Bank'. That's it, I thought – I'll be Stephanie Anne Lloyd!

The next step was speech therapy, for which I had to travel to Bury General Hospital because it was one of the few hospitals in the north of England to have a special computer program that was able to detect whether a voice was male or female. I used to sit in front of a computer screen with a microphone and follow a pattern which would be displayed on the screen. First a woman's voice would make a statement, and then I would have to try and copy it so that the computer could match up the patterns and analyse whether it was a woman or man speaking. For months it kept saying 'Male', but then miraculously one day the girl at the control panel in the other room came rushing out excitedly yelling, 'It's a girl! It's a girl!' I was so thrilled that I hugged her and we danced around the room yelling, 'It's a girl! It's a girl!' like a couple of demented new fathers whose wives have just given birth! But getting my voice to sound like a woman's to a computer was the least of my worries in this connection, for then I had to start learning about inflection, how to start a sentence and how to end it because – women's voices go up at the end of a sentence, whereas men's go down.

Learning to be a woman was difficult and very confusing. For example, men are allowed to sit with their legs apart. When men are introduced to each other, they're trained to shake hands firmly and look each other straight in the eye. If women do that they could be perceived as issuing an invitation! Then there were all those zips and hooks and buttons which seemed to do up in a different way. I even had to learn how to gesticulate in a feminine manner and to play with ear-rings and necklaces and twiddle my hair!

There was one unexpected benefit to all this tuition, though, because I actually found my new skills coming in very useful in the board room or at a particularly tense meeting. Previously I'd always been fairly commanding in meetings – my problem was I was a bit of a table thumper when I got annoyed. Now, however, I discovered the art of just waiting, saying nothing and looking round the table in order to bring a room under control. I soon discovered it was just as effective as banging your fist.

When Stuart, my chairman, had insisted I stay on, he had said that he would break the news about me gradually. First he would tell the board. A few months later he'd tell the subsidiary board. Then he'd let management and executives in on the secret, and finally, he'd make an announcement to the staff a few months before I left to have the operation. In this way everyone would have an opportunity to get used to the idea before it became *fait accompli*. Once again we decided to explain this highly complicated situation by simply repeating the story I had told the children, about an incurable disease necessitating hormone treatment which would transform me into a woman. When everyone in the company had been informed they were all very supportive. If people gossiped and speculated behind my back, it was never made known to me. The only person who didn't seem particularly happy was the Production Director, Nick Bellamy, with whom I'd never got on, but he of all people should have been over the moon because he got the MD's job in my place.

At that point, everything in my life seemed well. The date of my operation was drawing nearer, I'd been assured that my job was secure, and I was finally beginning to master many of the things I needed to learn to be an effective and credible woman. The one sad aspect was that I didn't get to see my children as often as I would have liked, but Marylin and I wrote to each other regularly and frequently spoke on the phone. Apart from that, the only cloud on my personal horizon was the prospect of having to tell my parents what I was about to do. Following my divorce, I'd been down to stay with them for odd weekends and our relationship had been fairly good, but in my heart I knew that the moment I told them the truth all hell would break loose. I kept putting the moment off. First I convinced myself it would be better if I wrote to them; then I changed my mind and decided phoning would be better. This went on for weeks as I dithered about how best to break the news. Finally, I knew there was no alternative: I had to visit them and tell them the truth face to face.

I left work on the Friday evening and drove straight down to Harpenden. As usual they were pleased to see me. That night I didn't say a word – somehow I couldn't bring myself to ruin the whole weekend. But by Saturday evening I was a nervous wreck. I said I wanted to talk to them, and we all went into the lounge. We sat for several moments in uncomfortable silence as they no doubt wondered what to expect, while I was playing for time and wondering how – and where – to begin. Eventually I took a deep breath and simply said: 'There's no easy way to tell you what I'm going to tell you. And there's no way I can prepare you for the shock of what I'm going to say.' And then I told them everything.

I don't think they believed what they were hearing. They were in such a state of shock they could only sit there staring blankly at me. Dad's first words, when they eventually came, were: 'What are our friends and neighbours going to say?' If it wasn't so sad I might have been tempted to laugh; it was precisely the kind of inane remark people make when they're too upset to think what they're saying – though I'm convinced Dad hadn't meant it the way it must have sounded. Then, after several moments of strained silence, he said: 'If you do this, I'll disinherit you.'

My eyes travelled back and forth between the faces of my parents. I couldn't think of anything to say. It was obvious from the look on Mum's face that she was devastated. In my heart I knew I had always been special to her, as sons often are to their mothers in a way they're not to their fathers, and I'm sure the shock was far worse than it would have been were it my sister telling them she wished to become a man.

I looked once more at my father. I knew there was no possible way I could make him understand. Having been brought up in their faith, I was all too well aware of the Jehovah's Witness belief that men were the superior sex. Dad simply couldn't comprehend why a member of that sex should want to give up his superiority, and not only give it up, but actually undergo surgery in order to become a member of what he had been trained to believe was an inferior sex.

There was nothing left to say and nothing that I could do, so I went to bed and lay there in the dark, hating the way I was hurting them, but knowing that things had gone too far for me to turn back now. I didn't sleep, partly because my numb brain wouldn't allow me to and partly because I could hear my mum crying all night long. In the morning we all looked dreadful. Cutting my visit short by several hours, I told them I was leaving right away. Once again we went through another traumatic scene that seemed to mirror grotesquely the one we'd played years before when I told them I was marrying Marylin. They begged and pleaded with me to change my mind. Mum clung to me at the door, sobbing, while Dad stood angry and mute in the background. I had no doubt that Dad would never forgive me and that his righteous anger and indignation would see him through the weeks and months that lay ahead. But

Mum? Without doubt it must have been the worst thing she's ever had to endure.

I drove away with the tears pouring down my cheeks. It wasn't a case of wishing I could change my mind – it was too late for that now. I'd tried everything to avoid this decision, and nothing had worked. If my parents thought, as they'd indicated before I left, that 'I could always go and see another doctor and it would be all right again', they were grasping at straws. I suppose what made it even worse was that there had never been any sign of my being effeminate. With my crazy past they had every reason to believe that I was nothing less than a red-blooded male. Could anyone understand what a shock it must have been for them?

Despite being deeply saddened and distressed by this latest breach between me and my parents, as my body took on more and more of a woman's shape I began to be filled with a sense of wonder and awe. For more than thirty years it had looked just like every other man's, and now, suddenly, it was totally differ-ent. Sometimes, however, my feelings were strangely ambi-valent. I found it difficult to look at myself in the mirror unclothed, though I didn't mind if I was half-dressed. I could cope with the top half looking like a woman if I couldn't see that the bottom half still looked like a man, but it was too bizarre to see the two halves of me together. I was an in-betweeny, neither one thing nor the other, and though on the one hand it was frustrating and at times even made me feel freakish, there were also many occasions when my situation gave me cause for amusement.

One of them was during a regular three-monthly trip to London during which I had to dress and behave as a woman. By now I was becoming fairly confident with my new 'image' and thought I was a rather convincing 'lady'. It was a hot, sticky summer's day and I was perspiring (I no longer 'sweated' like a man) as I caught a taxi from the station to the hotel. On arrival, the cabbie unceremoniously dumped my luggage on the pave-ment, leaving me to struggle into the hotel with it myself. Grumbling to myself, I staggered into the reception and rang the bell for attention, barely taking notice of a guy standing in the reception area staring at me. A few moments later the man approached with a drink in each hand and drawled in an unmistakable Canadian accent: 'Hi, honey, you look like you could really use this.'

'Well,' said I, 'that's the most novel introduction I've heard yet!' If the man had offered to buy me a drink I would have refused. Instead he'd pre-empted a potential refusal by buying it anyway and offering it to me at the very moment I was most in need. I had to admire that.

That evening we enjoyed a very pleasant meal together, which he insisted on paying for. Thankfully, my companion proved to be a stimulating conversationalist and not in the least pushy, although to be fair if he had been he would have been on a hiding to nothing. As it was, I retired to my room alone and spent the night reflecting not only on how nice it was to be completely accepted as female, but also on the novelty of having a man buy dinner for me!

What with work, my thrice-weekly date with Betty's dreaded needle and my shopping jaunts and 'lessons in being a lady' from Sandra, life was fairly busy and therefore time passed quickly. But as my big day grew closer and closer I felt an increasing sense of excitement and trepidation.

After Marylin had moved south, she kindly allowed me to take the children on holiday each summer. Determined to make the most of our stay together, we all had a wonderful time. Those days remain in a corner of my memory as the brightest spots in those two and a half years before my 'change'. The previous year we'd had a canal holiday, which was great fun, and though I'm sure Stephen, Andrew and Becky couldn't help but be aware of the physical transformation that was taking place in me, to their credit they never once asked an awkward or embarrassing question. In fact, the only time the subject was raised was when Stephen watched me hauling our cases out of the car boot and shyly said: 'Let me take those, Dad. Remember, you're going to be a woman soon.'

'Oh, my God!' I thought, gulping in surprise. 'I wonder if he's really thought about what he's saying?' Was it nothing more than a purely spontaneous remark? Or could it be that Stephen was already coming to terms with what was about to happen to me?

This year, my very last as their father, we were going to have another holiday together just a few weeks before my operation. We decided not to do the canal trip again, but spent the time going out to the theatre, shows and meals. All too soon it was time for them to return home. I drove them to Manchester Piccadilly Station on the Sunday morning to catch their train, desperately trying to conceal the tears in my eyes and the lump in my throat. I loaded them up with food, drink, chocolates and reading material, kissed them all goodbye and then walked down the platform, not daring to look back over my shoulder for fear I'd break down. As always it was heart-wrenching to see them go. Had I but known it was going to be the very last time I would ever see them again, I don't think I could ever have been able to let them out of my sight.

Just before Christmas I wrote a memo to the staff, informing them that I would be leaving the company on 23 December 1983, to be replaced as marketing director on 5 January 1984 by Miss Stephanie Anne Lloyd. It continued:

... and whilst you will, no doubt, notice many differences in appearance, our management styles are identical. Miss Lloyd will face a difficult time next year and I know she will appreciate all the help you can give her. I sincerely hope that this unavoidable change will not cause any difficulties, and whilst both you and she may be somewhat apprehensive on the 5th, I hope that it will not take long to establish a relaxed and comfortable working relationship.

Finally, may I thank you personally for the many messages of support I have received. Whilst it was never my intention to stay when this time arrived, I am now deeply grateful to Stuart Wallis for his persuasion and support, and pleased that his prediction of people's reactions has proved to be so accurate.

Having taken care of everything I could possibly take care of, I left my office for the last time as Keith Michael Hull. The moment I got home, I stripped off my business suit for ever. After packing a case with my female clothes I took a bath, then poured myself a drink. At long, long last my years of torment and waiting were finally over.

STEPHANIE

7
BORN AGAIN

On 12 September 1983 I was born again – a fully grown woman. I didn't want to hear the gory details about my rebirth, but I couldn't avoid knowing what was involved.

The procedure which was literally to transform my life would take around nine hours. During that time the surgeon, Mr Philip, would use every ounce of his skill delicately to eradicate every visible physical trace of my former male self. He would remove the testicles from the scrotal sac and the tissue and muscle from within the penis, leaving only a shortened urethra and the outer penile skin intact. Then he would create a false vagina approximately ten to eleven inches in length, which he would line with the penile skin before packing it with surgical dressings to minimize the chances of my new vagina caving in. Utilizing the penile skin in this way would mean that, as the nerve-endings were still present, I would be capable of enjoying normal sexual intercourse as a woman. And while I would not possess a clitoris as natural women do, it was still possible, I was told, for me to have an orgasm.

It's a common fallacy that male-to-female transsexuals are homosexual by nature, but that's rarely if ever the case. Sexual intercourse was the last thing on my mind, because I'd never been the slightest bit interested in men and certainly didn't envisage that situation changing now. All I wanted was to look like a woman and to be a woman; it was immaterial to me whether that included being able to function like a woman in a sexual respect. Having said that, I couldn't help but find it ironic that I, the one person who had once worked so hard to perfect the art of clitoral stimulation through oral sex, should now be incapable of achieving any satisfaction myself this way.

If I have inadvertently oversimplified the enormous skill that such surgery requires, giving the impression that anyone with a Black and Decker drill and sewing kit could accomplish this miracle, then I apologise to the surgical and nursing team. It was indeed an extremely long, dangerous and highly complicated operation. Perhaps it's a testament to Mr Philip's exceptional skill that, though I've had examinations since then, not one doctor has ever been able to detect the seam....

'Stephanie! Stephanie!'

I was vaguely aware of a gentle voice tugging at my consciousness. I tried to open my eyes but my eyelids were weighed down. I felt as if I was floating in a long, dark, warm tunnel and really didn't want to wake up. Then, having satisfied themselves that I was all right, the nursing staff allowed me to drift back into a heavily sedated sleep for the next two or three days.

My first conscious recollection was of waking up to find Mr Philip sitting on the edge of my bed, gently stroking my hand. 'Hello, Stephanie.' Such simple words, but oh, the relief I felt at hearing them! I managed to smile back at the man who had spoken them, for I knew from his expression that my transformation into a woman had been a complete success. I was exultant. I'd come through and now I was truly a woman. There was nothing left to fear. As tears of pure joy streamed down my face I could only look into my 'creator's' eyes and pray that he understood my gratitude. This man had given me the most precious gift on earth; he'd given me back my life. There were no adequate words to convey what that meant to me.

'I don't need to tell you again that your new life will be far from easy, Stephanie. When you leave here you will encounter prejudice and rejection to a degree you have never known. Yet, no matter how difficult the road ahead may prove to be, always remember that *you are a girl in a million!*' Those words have stayed for ever in my head. For, though Mr Philip was right and I have encountered just about every reaction it is possible to predict – and even some that aren't, when people have treated me like a pervert or a freak – those words have given me the strength, the pride and the dignity to hold my head up high.

The mood of joy stayed with me for the next few days, even as I lay wired to an ECG monitor with an assortment of catheters, bags, drips and tubes snaking in and out of my body. A few days later the sedatives were withdrawn and I was encouraged to get out of bed and start learning how to use this wonderful, unfamiliar new body I now occupied. As I hobbled the few yards across my room to my en suite bathroom in a determined effort to test out my new mechanics, I couldn't help laughing at the sight of myself in the mirror. For someone who had taken two years of deportment lessons I made a very credible John Wayne! As I attempted to relieve myself I was in stitches, both figuratively and literally, at my complete inability to control the direction of the flow. As a man, of course, I'd been used to standing up to pee, but clearly as a woman that just wouldn't do at all! The entire situation struck me as so comical that, despite the stitches and the pain, I was doubled up with laughter.

On the following Saturday – the sixth day of my new life – Mr Philip came in specially to remove the vaginal pack. If I'd thought electrolysis the most painful thing on earth, it was a breeze compared to the sensation of having your entire interior dragged outside. Obviously, too, I was tense and nervous as he went to work, wondering what else might be removed or dislodged by this excruciating and highly embarrassing excavation work. To my delight, Mr Philip's handiwork survived the experience.

When I was ten days old I was allowed to go home. Obviously I wasn't in a fit condition to drive myself from London to Lancashire, so I had to rely on cabs and planes to deliver me safely home. The journey was horrendous, as every lump and bump in the road made itself painfully obvious to my tender, swollen genitals. But the pain and discomfort were tempered by the sweet glow of comfort, contentment and peace I had felt since the first conscious moment of my rebirth. If I had likened meeting Marylin to coming out of a monochromatic world, seeing that same world through Stephanie's eyes was like looking at life in glorious, dazzling technicolour. Had everything always been this bright? Or did it merely seem so because I was so grateful to be alive?

Back home, I settled into my new life, taking it easy while I recuperated. Every day for the first month. I had to use plastic dilators in order to ensure the future elasticity of my vagina, and though it was undignified and awkward I could never fail to see the funny side as well. Sandra visited me once or twice and remarked at my new-found serenity and joy. Trevor called too, inviting me to stay with him at Christmas – an invitation I was only too grateful to accept.

I telephoned my parents to make sure they were all right, but since I had no wish to upset them further by speaking of things they had no desire to hear of, my conversation was stilted. Then, to my complete astonishment, my mother asked me if I would like to spend Christmas with them. I could hardly believe my ears, particularly as it was the very last thing I had expected them to do. Now I was really in a dilemma; on the one hand I had already accepted Trevor's offer and had been really looking forward to seeing him again. At the same time I knew I couldn't possibly turn down this opportunity for a reconciliation with my parents. So, despite the fact that my parents' faith would inevitably mean a fairly cheerless, possibly even tense, Christmas, the very fact that they had extended the invitation filled me with so much gratitude and hope that I couldn't possibly refuse.

Unfortunately, my optimism was short-lived. For after a long, tiring journey I was greeted by a mother who, while she tried valiantly to put me at my ease, clearly felt uncomfortable, and a father who still doggedly persisted in calling me Keith! My heart sank as I realized that this attempt at a reconciliation was at my mother's insistence and, though it stemmed from the purest of motives, I wished she hadn't bothered. Dad's barely disguised hostility towards me confirmed what I'd always suspected: he was never going to accept me as Stephanie, and this Christmas was going to be the worst kind of trial by ordeal.

Dear Auntie Elsie came over for a meal and tried hard to act normally in order to force my father's hand, but each day was worse than the one before. We were obviously not communicating, and I don't know which was worse – my father's implacable face or my mother's haunted, imploring eyes. We returned Auntie Elsie's visit, but it was all a horrid pretence. Unable to bear it any longer, I made my excuses and left. I couldn't watch my own and my mother's hopes disintegrate any more.

The roads were dreary and uncharacteristically empty as I made my way north, but I hardly noticed; all I was aware of was the bitter ache in my heart and the lump in my throat. On a whim, as I passed through Bolton I decided to stop off at an animal sanctuary and find some lonely little pup in desperate need of love. Despite the fact that I'd half expected it, I was feeling so abandoned, mistreated and desolate myself that somehow the only way I could conceive of easing my anguish was through taking care of someone more unfortunate than myself.

As I surveyed the sixteen dogs caged in individual concrete pens, pathetically awaiting either salvation or death, my heart sank. I wished I could take them all. Tails wagged in an hysterical bid for affection as dog after dog sprung to the front of its cage, yelping and barking to get my attention. But all I could see was one sad, lonely bitch who looked to be an odd cross between alsatian and whippet, shivering and shaking at the back of her cage as if she knew she didn't stand a chance. As I read the card on her pen revealing that she would be put to sleep the following day, something tugged at my heart. Instinctively I knew this was the dog for me. Here was someone who knew all about suffering, pain and rejection, and therefore had a great deal in common with me. I discovered later that she had been starved and then cruelly whipped with a chain before being abandoned.

I carried Sheba to my car where she immediately cowered in terror beneath the seat. On the way home I stopped off to buy food, bowls and a lead, and then felt wretched when I saw that, fearing more punishment, she immediately wet herself at the sight of the lead. It was six months before I was able to win her confidence enough to house-train her, but Sheba has repaid all my patience, time and effort a hundredfold.

The day finally arrived when I was to return to work. For Keith it would be a familiar journey, one he had taken for the past seven years. But Keith was no more, and for Stephanie this would be a first.

In order to make my arrival less spectacular, I'd arranged to go in a little later than everyone else and for Sandra to come to my house to help me with my make-up so that I would look my best. There was much twitching of venetian blinds as I walked across the car park. It was only natural that people should be curious to see what I looked like, I supposed, but the reception staff behaved as efficiently and normally as ever. When I walked into my office I was staggered to see that it was full of flowers and telegrams from people wishing me well – including Stuart, the chairman. My return was greeted with less prurient interest and more generosity and warmth than I had anticipated, and I was grateful for the chance to be allowed to ease myself back into the job.

At the beginning of February 1984 I attended an exhibition in Paris with Nick Bellamy, who had been appointed MD in my place. During one of my regular calls to my secretary I was alarmed to hear that two reporters from the *Daily Mirror* had been snooping around and, having been refused either access to or comment from any of the directors, they'd stooped to hanging around in the local pubs to see what they could learn from our shop floor workers. I wondered how they might have got hold of the story and soon it became obvious: one of my very own staff had betrayed me to the press – and for a price of just £100.

I caught the first available flight back to Manchester and drove straight from the airport to our family home, Wynthorpe, which I had moved back into when Marylin had left. I parked in the drive close to the front door and was just unlocking the boot when I suddenly became aware of a scuffling sound. I looked up to see several people bursting through the bushes into the garden, and was momentarily blinded by the flash bulbs of what seemed to be dozens of cameras. Bewildered by the questions that were being thrown at me, I didn't know what to do. I was trapped outside my home and there was nowhere to run. I had no option other than to stand my ground and say something that would make them go away.

'Look, guys, under the terms of my contract of employment I'm not allowed to give press interviews. However, if you're patient I'll try to ensure that the company issue an official statement outlining all the details of my situation.'

'Let's have a picture, then!' one of the mob yelled. It was just like being at the mercy of a pack of baying hounds. Why did they want me to pose for pictures? They'd already taken enough to fill an album! Eventually it became clear that they were determined not to go away empty-handed so, against my better judgement, I agreed to pose for two formal pictures in return for their promise that they would omit all details of my former wife and my children. The moment I was able to escape into the safety of my home, I locked the door and phoned Stuart.

'You did the right thing, Stephanie,' he said. 'I think I'm going to have to discuss this with the board before any of us says anything more.'

Stuart's calm handling of the situation did much to relieve my anxiety. If the paper knew they would be issued with an official statement, they'd hardly print a story on what they'd got so far. At least that's what I thought. Unfortunately, unbeknown to me, one member of staff had given the *Daily Mirror* a new angle by inadvertently mentioning that I'd been flown home, desperately ill, from the Far East three years before and had been undergoing hormone treatment ever since. The *Mirror* wasn't about to let go of a story on which it believed it had a world-wide exclusive, and so it simply put two and two together and came up with five.

That Sunday night, as the *Mirror*'s presses rolled out the following day's paper, I was besieged by newspapermen all wanting to get in on the act. During the early hours of Monday morning I was even woken by reporters from the *Manchester Evening News* who were screaming through the letter box at me to come down and give them the story too.

I hadn't seen the papers before I left home for work, but I wasn't allowed to remain in ignorance for long. On Monday, 6 February 1984 I was front page news. Under the banner headline 'MIRROR EXCLUSIVE' screamed the words: 'AMAZING SEX CHANGE BY THE BOSS'. The entire front page was taken up with 'before' and 'after' pictures of me, alongside a totally erroneous story which was continued on the whole of page three. I couldn't believe my eyes. If it hadn't been so awful, I might have laughed. After all, all I had wanted was simply to be allowed to live in peace as a woman, and now here I was a page three girl!

. The office was crawling with British and foreign journalists who, desperate for news and frustrated by our refusals to co-operate, had resorted to accosting every single member of the company who might be able to give them some juicy little detail to boost their circulations. Confounded by the sheer intensity of the media's interest, none of us knew quite how to cope. In retrospect I believe we all handled it very badly, but at the time we did what seemed the most sensible thing. Instead of issuing a statement to the press, the company chose to remain silent and I was advised to go away and hide for a week in the hope that things would die down. Unfortunately, the lack of information only fanned the flames. Desperate for *any* kind of story, true or false, the press decided to speculate.

The company suggested I get right out of the country for a week or so, but I preferred to take a week's break in the Lake District – at least that way I would be able to keep in touch. The press coverage continued throughout the entire week I was away as newspaper after newspaper became more fanciful and sleazy. If it hadn't been so tacky and upsetting, I might have been amused; for if I'd truly done everything they claimed, I'd be more than a mere story – I'd be an epic!

At the end of the week Stuart called and asked me to meet him and Nick at the Last Drop Hotel in Bolton to 'discuss the present situation'. I had no idea what to expect, but I was beginning to feel decidedly apprehensive. The moment I looked at Stuart's face, I realized with a sinking heart what was in store. Hestair couldn't handle the publicity. My fears were confirmed when Stuart informed me, albeit regretfully, that my situation had now become too hot for them to handle. Moreover, they were afraid of the possible reaction from the company's institutional shareholders. To save the embarrassment of being fired I resigned and my resignation was promptly accepted. Stuart simply said,

'I'm sorry, Stephanie,' and I believe he really was. 'But we'd like to invite you to remain on as an external consultant if you're willing to do that.'

'I'm sorry, too, Stuart,' I replied. 'But on reflection, I feel it would be better for us all if the break is completely clean.'

Once again, as so often before in my life, I drove back home in tears. I must have cried so often in that car it's a wonder the interior wasn't rusty from damp. If only I'd followed my earlier instinct and left twelve months before. At least then I would have been able to set up my own company and be in charge of my own destiny.

That night I telephoned Marylin to break the awful news. She was furious with me, because the family were still dependent on me financially. Without a job, or even any prospects of a job, how would I be able to support them all? I understood that it was more than she could take, but I was also saddened and upset. It was a disaster for her, but it was a catastrophe for me. What was I supposed to do now?

That phone call marked the beginning of the end of my relationship with Marylin, and from that moment things quickly began to go sour. In an attempt to protect Marylin's and the children's financial security, I suggested that it might be wise if I signed all our joint assets over to her. A court hearing, at which the legal formalities would be taken care of, was duly set for several weeks hence.

Though my salary had been a good one, the cost of running two households, together with the additional expenses of beauty treatment and a whole new wardrobe meant that I'd never been able to save. When I counted up all my assets I had seventy-eight pence, the clothes I stood up in, and one loyal, faithful, dependent dog. I had lost my job, my salary, my car, my family and most of my friends. For the first time in my entire life I stood completely alone. And yet, though some might find this difficult to believe, apart from my immediate practical problems I had never been more at peace with myself or more content.

The most pressing problem as far as I was concerned was how I was going to be able to afford food for Sheba. On a recommendation I contacted a solicitor, Richard Holman, who I hoped would represent me at the court hearing. It was three days before he could see me. During those three days Sheba and I existed solely on milk and bread that I was able to get delivered on credit from the local milkman.

If I took Sheba for a walk, I'd find my footsteps being dogged by hordes of young children who would follow me, chanting names. It brought home to me the fact that I was considered a freak not only by those who knew me but also by those who didn't. The thought occurred to me that, were I suddenly able to skip back a century or so, I'd undoubtedly have been exhibited in a freak show. But were modern-day attitudes to people like me any more enlightened or humane?

Three days later, and by now all but destitute, I visited Richard Holman at his office. 'Look, I'd better tell you right now, I have no money, no job and no immediate prospects of a job, so I don't know how I'm going to pay you,' I told him frankly.

'Tell me about yourself,' Richard instructed. By the time I'd finished he looked both interested and doubtful. 'You must have *some* money,' he said.

'None at all,' I assured him.

He then began to question me about my car, my house, my bank accounts and so on. By the time I'd answered all his questions he was sitting back in his chair with a totally incredulous look on his face. 'You really *don't* have anything, do you?' Without further ado, Richard picked up the telephone, contacted Social Services and, after much opposition, managed to extract an emergency payment of £25 for me. 'Don't worry about our fees,' he said, 'I'm sure you'll qualify for Legal Aid.'

I was flabbergasted at the sincerity of his interest and concern. Richard's firm, Foyster's, weren't some tinpot little solicitors but a large practice that didn't normally deal with Legal Aid cases. But, as I soon discovered, Richard's concern stemmed from a genuine belief in justice and, despite my desperate straits, he treated me with exactly the same respect as he did all his clients. Now, with the princely sum of £25 in my pocket, I was at least able to buy food for Sheba and myself.

A few weeks later Richard accompanied me to the court hearing at Bolton. Marylin had made the trip from Devon to be there, but she refused either to look at me or to speak to me, leaving her barrister to address me on her behalf before the hearing commenced.

'You're still prepared to sign all your assets to your ex-wife?' he said.

'Yes,' I replied. 'Though I would like to keep one or two things, of course.'

'Oh. Like what?'

'Well, I'm going to need a bed – and then there are one or two personal things that belonged to my parents.'

The barrister looked put out. Signalling me to wait where I was, he rejoined Marylin for a whispered discussion. Then he returned to us.

'No, I'm sorry. She doesn't want you to have a bed.'

I didn't believe him! We had such a large house, and there were at least four or five single beds and a couple of doubles.

Although we haggled and bartered, the actual hearing itself was very brief. I had insisted on retaining possession of an antique sideboard that had belonged to my aunt, simply because I knew my aunt would be furious if I allowed Marylin to take it. But Marylin's attitude had me totally confused. I was handing just about everything I owned to her, including our house, which was worth about £75,000 and only carried a small mortgage, and the majority of our belongings. Why was she doing this to me? Particularly when she knew that the moment I had signed those papers I would be destitute.

But in my heart, I knew the answer to my questions. Marylin had finally had to confront Stephanie in the flesh – something she simply could not cope with. All the friendliness of the past few years, the phone calls and the chats, she'd only been able to handle because she had convinced herself I was still Keith. Now she had the evidence of her own eyes that Keith no longer existed, and I believe that was more than she could bear.

Within days I received a letter from Marylin's solicitors listing all the items that appeared to be missing from the house – things like 'one saucepan', 'four scatter cushions', etc. The whole thing was so petty that I could hardly believe it.

Naturally I assumed that I would be able to stay on living in the house until a buyer was found, but even that was denied me, for within a week or so I was served with an eviction order. The bank froze my (empty) account, I was unable to use my credit cards because I was without the financial means to pay my debts. Every which way I turned led to a dead end. What on earth was I supposed to do? I had felt badly enough about losing my job, my entire career, but the money aspect of it hadn't really affected me. Somehow, I had thought I might be able to buy a little hotel or something; but now that the reality of my situation was staring me in the face I was beginning to realize how naïve and over-optimistic I had been.

Contrary to what the press had reported in the past few weeks, having said the immortal words, 'Okay then, I'll resign', I hadn't received a single penny from Hestair. The whole thing seemed like some crazy farce to me. This couldn't possibly be happening to me! But it was.

Still, I was convinced I'd soon be able to find myself another job. I'd been headhunted many times during my years at Hestair; there were lots of companies who would be eager, and even grateful, to acquire a person with my skills, experience and knowledge. It never occurred to me that, just like a stack of dominoes, once one part of your world starts to tumble down the rest of it is not very far behind.

More immediately, however, there were other problems to attend to. With eviction hanging over my head, I had to find somewhere to live. Once again, Richard came to my rescue by managing to get a two-week extension on the eviction order. Meanwhile, the £25 emergency payment I'd received had run out and, though I had contacted dozens of employment agencies and sent my c.v. to whoever I thought might be interested, I hadn't had so much as an acknowledgement, let alone the prospect of an interview.

With only Sheba for company I walked all the way into town and signed on at the dole office. *That*, as anyone who's ever been on the dole will undoubtedly confirm, is such a horrendously humiliating experience that I could hardly bring myself to go back the following week. My face had become so well known that wherever I went I was bound to attract unwelcome attention. To be as notorious as I had become was bad enough, but to have people staring and pointing at me in the dole queue, and knowing that they probably believed all the stories about the huge sums of money the media reported I'd received as a pay-off, was too awful for words.

The strain and pressure were beginning to take their toll, so when I visited my doctor for a routine check-up and he suggested an alternative to being on the dole, I was only too grateful to accept.

'After all,' he explained 'if the publicity and all your other problems are affecting you this much, you have every right to be considered temporarily unfit for work. And although that means you won't qualify for dole money, you will be able to claim sick relief.'

Despite the fact that this meant I'd actually be £1 a week worse off, I was so relieved not to have to face the dole queue again that it was worth it to me.

Then at last my job applications began to bring in a number of requests for interviews – but, despite my excellent track record, not for the right reason. It soon became apparent that I was only being invited because the interviewers were intrigued. They knew who I was, of course. With all the publicity, how could they not? No one, however, seemed to be remotely inclined to employ me.

I spent several days thinking over my plans, finally reaching the conclusion that the only business I could now do well in would be one in which who I was – as well as what I was – would be not a liability but an asset. Meanwhile I needed to buy myself a car, as the prospect of continually having to use public transport and being exposed to all those hostile and curious stares was more than I could bear. Even an old banger would do, but I had nothing to sell. My only possession was Aunt Elsie's antique sideboard, and as I couldn't bear to part with it permanently I wondered whether there might be some way to secure a loan against it. I picked up the Yellow Pages and rang the first number I came across to seek advice on how to go about organizing a valuation.

'We can't help you here,' the friendly young man at the end of the telephone said, 'but there's a man I know who is very knowledgeable and could advise you on its worth. I can arrange for him to come and see you tomorrow if you like.' I said that would be fine.

The next evening, Robert arrived at my door. He was not very tall, rather thin and very well-preserved for a man whom I judged to be somewhere in his sixties. I invited him in, made a pot of tea and then asked him to evaluate the sideboard. But to my consternation, he seemed far more interested in evaluating me!

Bob, as he asked me to call him, was obviously a wealthy man, though very much the public school type who did not believe in flaunting either his wealth or status. He was well-bred, knowledgeable, intelligent and interesting, and I couldn't help liking him. To be honest, though, it never occurred to me that he could be interested in me. I had been a woman for such a short time that I still wasn't aware of the things women intuitively know about men. In retrospect I can see now that for Bob it seemed the ideal situation. Here I was, a divorced woman living on her own and therefore eminently available. I was more intrigued by the fact that he gave no indication of knowing who and what I was, and that was a novelty to me.

After giving me his estimation of the sideboard's current value, Bob seemed strangely disinclined to leave. The following day I received an enormous bouquet of flowers from him. The next day, another bouquet arrived, and the next and the next, until there was only the dog's bowl left without a floral arrangement. By that time I was beginning to panic. Should I telephone him and thank him, or should I wait for the inevitable call? On the one hand, Bob had boosted my ego enormously at a time when nobody else wanted to have anything to do with me. On the other, what would happen when he found out about me?

Finally he telephoned and, despite having expected it, I found I was still totally unprepared when he invited me to have dinner with him. I declined. It was impossible – I couldn't possibly get involved with this man, as nice as he was. But I reckoned without Bob's persistence. He refused to take no for an answer, though he eventually settled for the promise of a drink. Obviously, he wasn't going to let me off his hook that lightly. So, knowing that I was in a tricky situation, I resolved to tell him the truth. I arranged with Bob to collect me at home that evening, suggesting that we drive out to a pub called the Thomas Dutton at Edgerton, just two miles across the moors that divided Darwen from Bolton.

I spent the rest of the day worrying about what I should wear, selecting and discarding a variety of different outfits. *Why not just turn up in jeans and sweater?* I asked myself. *You're only going to tell the man the truth – why bother to get dressed up?* But six-thirty found me bathed, made up, dressed to kill and nervously alternating between checking my lipstick and my watch.

When we arrived at the pub I sat in the darkest corner I could find, hoping and praying that nobody would recognize me or stare. I hadn't been out in ages, and soon the combination of that novelty, Bob's easy conversation and the odd drink or two made me relax. Then he made his move.

'I'd very much like you to have dinner with me one evening, Stephanie,' Bob said.

Uh oh! I thought. *Here it is. How are you going to get out of this now? There's only one thing to do. You've been avoiding it long enough, but you're really going to have to tell him the truth now.* I opened my mouth, but no words came out.

'Em, I think I'll just pop to the ladies,' I said, taking the coward's way out. Once in the loo, I looked at my reflection in the mirror. *What's the matter with you?* I said to myself. *You've stood up in front of hundreds and delivered word-perfect speeches. You've appeared on TV, you're confident and self-assured. Just get on out there and* tell *him.*

With stiffened shoulders, I marched resolutely out into the

bar, walked across to the table and said to Bob: 'Right. I've got something to tell you. But ... first I'm going to put on my coat.'

Bob must have thought I was mad, but maybe he had first-hand experience of eccentrics, because he merely stood up and helped me into my coat with no more than a quizzical smile.

'Right. Now. You're not to say anything at all. Just sit there and listen. And when I leave, you mustn't follow me.'

Bob's mouth opened and closed like a goldfish as I launched myself into my tale. Thirty seconds later, having encapsulated my entire life story into that short period of time, I rushed out into the night. There was only one vital flaw in my plan: without a car, how the hell was I going to get home?

What a bloody fool you are, Stephanie! I berated myself as I began to tramp the long, weary road that snaked across the moors back to my home. Two cars passed me as I walked and both stopped to offer me a lift, but as each contained a solitary man I ignored the offers and walked on. I had covered almost half the distance when Bob's car pulled up behind me with a screech and he jumped out, wrenched open the passenger door and commanded me forcefully to get in.

I did. We drove back to my place in complete silence. When we arrived I got out, unlocked the front door and started to walk away, certain that I would never see this man again. Suddenly, Bob's arm reached out to grasp my shoulder and turn me round to face him. With a wry smile, he gently touched my tear-stained face and said: 'I think you're one hell of a courageous lady.' Then with a quick kiss he left.

Sheba lay waiting for me in the hall. Dropping my bag on to the floor, I lay down beside her with my arms around her neck and wept into her fur. At three in the morning, I awoke to find myself still there with Sheba curled up in my arms. I had an aching back and was stiff all over, but I felt better than I had done for weeks.

When I eventually got up, red-eyed and weary but otherwise in a far better mood, I was pottering around cleaning up the house before taking Sheba for her morning walk when the doorbell rang. On the doorstep stood yet another gigantic bouquet with a card attached which read: 'Just because you are you – Bob.' Poor Sheba's walk had to wait until I'd repaired the ravages of another bout of tears.

After that, Bob became a regular and very welcome visitor. We went out for meals, played backgammon together and took long walks with Sheba. Bob displayed an amazing amount of kindness towards me, and as he never attempted anything other than a quick goodbye kiss it wasn't long before I began to relax in his company and simply enjoy his friendship. I soon learned that he was sixty-three, successful and very seriously wealthy – and, predictably, also very much an unhappily married man. (It was years before I learned what most women seem to be born knowing: that all married men intent on having an affair are unhappily married.)

Soon enough the postponed eviction order was enforced. Once again I contacted Richard with the plea: 'What am I going to do now?'

What happened next was almost unbelievable. The Social Services offered to put me into a hostel for the homeless and to have Sheba put down. I was outraged.

'How can you suggest a thing?' I groaned. 'This dog is the only friend I have in the world!' I would have rather slept rough with Sheba than in comfort without her. Like most people, I didn't have a clue as to what my basic rights were. Fortunately, Richard did.

He contacted the local council and said: 'I'm coming over now with this girl and her dog. They will sleep on the council office steps and I'll be bringing a posse of reporters to record and publicize your callous attitude.'

Oh, the power of the press! It was just as if a magic wand had been waved, for in no time at all the council agreed to provide a roof over my head. I moved in immediately, and for the next few weeks the only time I emerged was either to potter around on my own in the garden or to take Sheba for a long walk with Bob.

I couldn't help growing more fond of Bob as he helped me to move into my new home at West Houghton, always appearing eager to help around the house and do odd little jobs for me. He even built a kennel for Sheba. And whilst part of me was rather nervous that he might want 'payment in kind', I was curiously drawn towards him. Without doubt, it was a weird situation to be in. I was thirty-seven years old and behaving like a shy little virgin. Which, of course, I suppose I was, in a way.

Then, one night, Bob took me out to dinner and ordered champagne to celebrate our having known one another for a whole month. When he took me home, we relaxed with another bottle that he'd left on ice, and as the hours gently passed in the warm and heady atmosphere Bob successfully and expertly seduced me. I couldn't believe that I had lost my virginity in the most romantic, gentle love-making I'd ever known. If I had been stone-cold sober, I'm sure I wouldn't have been able to go through with it. As it was I was relaxed, slightly drunk and my defences were definitely down. And, if I'm perfectly frank, I enjoyed this new experience of being seduced. If I had any momentary qualms, they came at the point of no return, when suddenly I feared that Mr Philip's handiwork might not stand up to the wear and tear!

The amazing thing was the difference in the actual quality of orgasm. As a man, I'd only ever experienced an orgasm that was totally centred on my loins; I had no idea that for a woman it's totally different. It was like dropping pebbles into a pond and watching the waves spread right across the water in ever-widening circles. Another strange difference intrigued me. Knowing what it was like to make love as a man, I was well aware that for most men all the affection and tenderness seems to come *before* their orgasm – or, to put it another way, for men orgasm is a full stop, whereas for women it's merely a comma, a prelude to a feeling that can become something much more. For me it was a totally incredible and beautiful experience, one that I couldn't possibly ever come to regret.

8
TRANSFORMATION

Following all the publicity, I had received several letters from complete strangers. One of these came from a transsexual called Caroline who lived in Chester. Caroline told me she was a qualified accountant, and offered to use her knowledge and expertise to help me with my financial affairs. By this time I was in debt up to my ears and being threatened with bankruptcy demands on all sides. The only reason it didn't happen was because it would have cost my creditors at least £700 to issue a writ, and as they knew it would be impossible to recoup even this small amount the whole exercise would have been like flogging a dead horse. It was to be several years before I was in a position to pay them all off.

By now things were just about as bad as they could get. Apart from the fact that I had a roof over my head and Bob and Sheba for company, my only real consolation was the feeling that things surely couldn't get any worse. As so often before I was to be proved wrong. I opened my mail one morning to find this letter from the Elders of the Jehovah's Witness Sect:

Dear Keith,
As indicated in reports in newspapers and on television, the Elders believe that you have gone astray in a moral sense and displayed conduct contrary to good Christian behaviour. As you were baptised originally into the Christian congregation as Keith Hull, a male, you are, therefore, unacceptable to God as a female.

You are hereby summoned to appear before a judicial committee of Elders to examine your behaviour and determine whether you have contravened the Jehovah's Law. Deuteronomy Chapter 22, Verse 5.

Although I had not been active in the religion for some time, I was, of course, aware of the very real consequences of being 'disfellowshipped', which is the same as excommunication in any other faith. Being excommunicated from the faith itself wasn't the problem; what worried me far more was the effect it would have on my parents: the moment I was banished from the faith I would, to all intents and purposes, be considered 'dead' by every Jehovah's Witness. And if that were to happen, I knew that because my parents' devotion to the faith was absolute, any faint hope I might have of effecting a reconciliation in the future would be gone forever.

Reluctantly, I concluded I had no choice but to attend. I obtained statements from every doctor and specialist I had seen, some of whom were even prepared to attend personally and swear that mine was a true medical condition and therefore, had been treated in the only way known to medical science. On that basis, the biblical verse in question (which forbids the wearing of male and female clothing by members of the opposite sex) simply was not relevant.

Immediately before the hearing I was informed that I could only take one companion into the hearing with me – and that person should be neither a doctor nor a legal representative. I was stumped. Clearly, the Elders of the faith saw only one way to deal with the bad publicity that they felt I had brought to their religion: dispose of me, and the publicity would disappear too. So on the appointed day I found myself seated alone before what can only be described as a kangaroo court of four grim-faced, self-appointed male 'judges'. What happened next can best be summed up by quoting the letter I subsequently sent to the committee:

Although informed on several occasions of my current medical condition which calls for the complete avoidance of stress and emotional upset, you have shown a total lack of empathy and have, by your actions, induced such conditions, thereby adversely affecting my health. I was amazed at your statement that 'as my problems are a result of my own actions I do not deserve any help'. Surely this is akin to refusing to give medical assistance to a child when it falls from a tree on the grounds that it should not have climbed it. I just cannot imagine that Jesus Christ would take such an attitude.

The charge that was formally read to me was that I 'had gone astray in a moral sense and displayed conduct contrary to good Christian behaviour', and yet you have been completely unable to provide a sound Biblical basis for such a judgement, rather, basing your argument on the fact that as I was baptised whilst legally male, I am unacceptable to God as a female.

From my own knowledge, both of the Bible's teachings and Society's, I am convinced that the way my case has been handled was fundamentally wrong and, therefore, is worthy of further investigation. Our religion teaches that Elders should show love, consideration and a desire to help the sick and needy back to full health, whether spiritually or physically. Yet your attitude towards me has been one of trying to dispose of a 'problem' as quickly and as quietly as possible. I believe it is obvious that I was tried and sentenced before the hearing took place.

The actual letter I wrote was, of course, far longer than that, and showed all the emotional anxiety and frustration that their callous attitude caused me to feel. I was more than disappointed – I was devastated. To appeal would be futile. I just had to find a way of accepting my excommunication. Far worse than that, however, would be having to come to terms with the fact that as far as all Jehovah's Witnesses including my parents, were concerned, I was now officially dead.

This last blow was almost too much to bear. Part of me simply felt like going to bed and wallowing in self-pity, but from the very beginning of my unemployed period I had been aware that the biggest danger was that I might grow lazy and undisciplined, finding that the less I had to do the less I would want to do. In order to combat this I imposed a very strict regimen upon myself, making sure that I got up early, took Sheba for her morning and afternoon walks, cleaned the house religiously and shopped whenever I needed to. The only people I saw or spoke to were Betty, Sandra, Richard Holman and Bob, who would pop over for a few hours every afternoon.

Although I had found a measure of inner peace and contentment, I was becoming more wary and insular, preferring to avoid all but the tried and tested few. Far better, I reasoned, not to get involved with strangers, who only seemed to want to indulge their prurient curiosity about me. However, when two lads, Steve and James, moved into the house next door and appeared not to have any idea who I was, or show any curiosity about my strange lifestyle, I soon found I could relax in their company and warm to their friendly, easy-going ways.

I stepped up my efforts to find a job, applying for every single marketing and sales director position advertised. My c.v. was a problem in that as all my experience had been achieved as Keith Michael Hull. Should I write a covering letter explaining why I was now calling myself Stephanie Anne Lloyd? Or should I simply substitute Stephanie's name for Keith's and let the recipients assume that I'd held my previous positions as a woman? I opted for the latter course, on the basis that explanations would only prove necessary immediately before any interviews I might be offered.

Shortly afterwards, a job agency contacted me and asked me in for an interview. Although at £17,000 the salary was far less than I was either used to or worth, in my present position it seemed like a fortune. The job was as marketing controller for the Co-op and, despite the fact that I made no secret of my background, the interviewer thought my credentials were perfect.

'As the position's been vacant for around six months,' said the interviewer, 'I imagine they'll want to see you as soon as possible. Why don't I telephone them right now to fix an appointment?'

'That's fine by me,' I replied. 'But I'd prefer you to make my identity and circumstances known to them *before* an interview.'

He picked up the phone. From the way the conversation went, it soon became obvious that the Co-op were more than interested in me. That is until the interviewer added: 'There's just one thing. The applicant is with me now and she's insisted that before any interviews are arranged I should inform you that she has recently been the subject of a great deal of publicity. Her name is Stephanie Anne Lloyd.'

I watched the expression on the interviewer's face turn from a smile to a frown. My heart sank. 'I see,' he commented before putting the receiver down. Hardly able to look me in the eye, he quietly said: 'I'm terribly sorry, but they simply don't want a transsexual.'

I went home alone to face the stark reality of my situation: despite my excellent track record, I wasn't just unemployed – I was unemployable. For several hours I was miserable. Then my fighting spirit returned – from that moment on, I resolved I would never again work for anyone but myself. All I had to do now was find something that I could set up on my own. Steve, James and Bob were unfailingly kind and did their utmost to keep my spirits up while I thought hard about my professional future and my financial problems.

I received an invitation from the BBC to take part in the *Midweek* programme presented by Libby Purves. This would entail spending a night in London with all expenses paid courtesy of the BBC. I had nothing to lose, and nothing else in my diary, so I decided to go along.

When I arrived at the hotel I was amazed to discover that I had been allocated an entire suite. This was luxury indeed! After indulging in a long, hot bath I dressed for dinner and went upstairs to the restaurant, arming myself with a book which I hoped would deter any unwanted advances. By now, I was beginning to be aware of the dangers inherent in being a woman on your own!

I was seated close to a table where two men were involved in what seemed to be a business discussion. To my surprise, as I finished my main course the waiter came over and relayed an invitation to join them in a glass of champagne. My first instinct was to say no, but a little voice in my head said: 'This is probably the last opportunity you'll have to drink champagne in the years to come. What harm can it do?' So I accepted their invitation.

Shortly afterwards, one of the men excused himself while I continued my discussion with his friend. It soon became apparent that my companion was nothing less than an Algerian multi-millionaire who seemed to have business interests in just about every field of commerce that existed. Much of his wealth, he informed me, had been inherited, but he had contributed greatly to his riches by his own business acumen. The conversation turned to me and, reluctant to reveal too much about myself, I talked a little about my background without going into any great detail.

As the evening wore on, the restaurant slowly emptied until finally there were just the two of us left behind. Omar (yes, that *really* was his name!) asked me what kind of music I liked best. Then he wandered over to the grand piano and, just like a scene in a romantic movie, began to play all my favourite melodies. His champagne, his charm and his exceedingly good looks were beginning to work their magic and I sat gazing at him with a mixture of pleasure, embarrassment and concern.

'I'd like to see more of you. You're not like any other woman I've ever known,' he said when he returned to the table. Half of me was thrilled to pieces, the other half appalled – and the irony of his last statement was not lost on me either! I only knew one way to handle this delicate, uncomfortable moment, and that was to tell Omar the truth about myself, just as I had done with Bob.

'I'm going to tell you something about myself,' I began. 'And when I've finished, I just want to say goodnight and leave. But first, let me thank you for a very enjoyable evening, for your hospitality, your kindness, and for the immense pleasure you have given me tonight.' Then I told him. And when I'd finished, I gathered up my book and my handbag and rushed straight to my room. My last backward glance registered his handsome face composed in an expression of total shock as he sat there staring after me, wide-eyed and open-mouthed.

Tears were welling in my eyes as I sped upstairs and into my room where I lay on my bed weeping my heart out in the certain knowledge that this was a scenario I would surely have to face over and over again in my life. And yet I could not, would not deceive anyone. How long I lay there I don't know, but my weeping was ultimately interrupted by a knock on the door. Miserably I rose from my bed, not even bothering to clean my mascara-stained cheeks or straighten my rumpled clothes. What did it matter how I looked? I opened my door and stared in amazement, for standing in front of me was Omar with a tray, two glasses and a magnum of champagne in an ice bucket.

'I've thought about it . . . and it doesn't make any difference,' was all he said in that husky, accented voice that was so sexy it reduced my knees to jelly. I cried again, but this time it was for an entirely different reason. Then we were lying on the couch together and my tears were forgotten as he began kissing and caressing me. When he had made love to me he carried me to the bed where we made love again – more slowly, tenderly and more satisfyingly than I had ever known. He stayed with me all night as we exchanged intimate confidences about ourselves and our lives. He wanted me to have breakfast with him, but my interview was scheduled so early that it was impossible.

'Then meet me for lunch,' he said imperiously.

The interview went well, though I thought it rather odd that I should be sharing the slot with a vicar and an escapologist who performed what I believe to be the only escape live on radio (which was all the more strange as there were only five of us present in the studio to witness such a feat!)

The moment the interview was over I rushed straight back to the hotel, left my baggage with the porter and called Omar on the house phone to let him know I had returned.

'Wait there,' was all he said. Within seconds he was bounding down the stairs and, to my utter stupefaction, hugging and kissing me in front of a hotel full of startled guests. I had feared that when the magic of the night and the champagne had worn off he might feel differently about me, but here he was, apparently just as keen.

We ate lunch in a small Italian restaurant, holding hands and gazing lovingly at each other. When we had finished, Omar looked deeply into my eyes and said: 'Stephanie, will you marry me?'

I was so astounded that I couldn't think of anything rational or even appropriate to say. All I could think of was a number of reasons why marrying Omar would be the worst possible thing I could do. He was a Muslim; I was a Christian. What would his parents say or do? It would be bad enough in their eyes for him to propose to someone he had known less than twenty-four hours, but how much worse would they feel knowing that I wasn't even legally a female? And what about the legal implications? Somehow I managed to garble out all the objections and protestations that presented themselves to me, but Omar refused to take no for an answer.

Finally, I said, 'Omar, I just can't make a decision of this magnitude at such short notice. You *have* to give me more time to think.'

Reluctantly, he agreed. Then, brightening slightly, he asked the waiter to bring over a piece of string which he wound around my finger triumphantly before declaring: 'Wait here. I'll be gone just a few moments.' Then he disappeared out into the street.

As I waited for Omar to return, I sipped my liqueur and gazed idly around me thinking, 'I don't believe this is happening to me.' My thoughts were in such a jumble that I'd lost the ability to think objectively or rationally. The only possible thing I could do was to play for time. I gave no thought to where Omar had gone, or for what reason but, true to his word, he was back within fifteen minutes saying: 'I know you've said you can't answer my question yet, but I would like you to do one thing for me.'

Not wanting to commit myself to something I knew nothing about, I demurred, but the more I resisted the more he pressed. In the end, I caved in. Immediately he produced a small, square box from his jacket pocket and with a flourish presented me with the most extravagantly gorgeous ring I had ever seen. Twenty-five individual, sparkling diamonds winked at me as I gazed in awe at the beautiful sunburst-patterned ring. It must have cost an absolute fortune, and I was totally lost for words.

Omar took my hand and placed the ring on my engagement finger. 'Please wear this ring – at least until you give me your decision.' I was so taken aback that I couldn't think of one single valid reason for either refusing or accepting, so I said nothing.

'Now,' he continued, 'you have said we do not know each other well enough. What I would like to suggest is that we go away for a few days together.' Without waiting for a reply (though, frankly, I was incapable of any coherent thought at all), Omar outlined his plan. We would fly to Geneva where he had some business to attend to, and then we would go anywhere in the world that I wanted to for a few days' relaxation, during which time we would get to know each other better.

'Omar!' I protested. 'That's impossible! I can't just disappear like that. I have a dog to take care of. I don't have my passport with me. I don't even have any suitable clothes with me!'

Like a man who considered such concerns a mere inconvenience, Omar brushed my protestations aside. 'You can call someone who will look after your dog. We can buy whatever clothes you are in need of. And we can fly to Manchester to your home to collect your passport.'

Omar's offer was sorely tempting after so many months of deprivation and loneliness, but somehow I knew that, if I accepted, I might well come to feel so obligated that things could get out of hand. Besides, while I was in his company I was patently unable to make rational decisions and in all probability would just be swept along by Omar's whims. So with a supreme effort at summoning up a determination I didn't really feel, I said no and insisted on returning home immediately. Despite being immensely disappointed, Omar insisted on taking me in his chauffeur-driven limousine to Heathrow and, after calling ahead for James to meet me at Manchester airport, saw me safely on to my plane.

Throughout the short flight I was in a state of profound shock. I just couldn't believe what had happened to me! It must be every young woman's dream to be swept off her feet by a dark, handsome, rich stranger – but that it should happen to *me*! If it wasn't for the enormous, expensive ring sparkling merrily on my finger, I would have been convinced the whole episode had been nothing more than a fantastic dream. When I told the tale to James he seemed just as stupefied as I, although he did tell me that I must be mad not to have gone. 'How absolutely typical of a man!' I thought.

Within days calls started arriving for me at James and Steve's house from all over the world. Wherever Omar went he telephoned me, and on every occasion he repeated his proposal. But despite hours spent walking amongst the fields surrounding West Houghton discussing my dilemma with an uncommenting Sheba, I still couldn't reach a decision.

My relationship with Bob had by this time settled into no more than platonic friendship. I'd been disillusioned and surprised when I had first discovered that he was married, but the hurt turned to outrage when he announced his objections to my spending so much time with James and Steve. By now, of course, I had realized that James and Steve were lovers, so it wasn't even as if they wanted anything from me that Bob might have felt was his. We still continued to be friends and to see each other in the afternoon, but I didn't want to continue a sexual relationship with him any more; and though I'm sure he wasn't happy about that, he knew me well enough by now not to complain. Besides, I wasn't particularly happy or impressed by the fact that, apart from our first date and the night when he'd seduced me, he never took me out. Like a lot of wealthy men, Bob didn't like parting with his money, and though it simply didn't occur to me to ask for financial help, the fact that it was never even offered spoke volumes.

Bob's extreme meanness was finally brought home to me on my birthday, when he came over for his usual afternoon game of backgammon and presented me with a package. Delighted that he had remembered, I tore the wrapping off to find that Bob had bought me a large wallet of coloured felt-tip pens! Convinced that this must be a joke and that his real present was to follow, I laughed. When I realized that this *was* my present, I didn't know whether to laugh or cry at the insult. I needed a set of felt tip pens like I needed a guided missile or another penis – either would have been about as much use to me in my present dire situation! Perhaps if I'd stayed with Bob until Christmas I'd have got the colouring book as well!

Still, it *was* my birthday, and Steve and James had very thoughtfully decided to take me out for a meal, so at least there was one bright event to look forward to. If only I'd known then just how memorable that birthday would prove to be! Before we left, two significant events occurred. The first was a whole vanload of flowers. The second was the arrival of a reporter from the *Manchester Evening News*. I had confided the details of my meeting with Omar to only about six trusted friends, and yet here was the *Manchester Evening News* begging for more details! Once again I had been betrayed by somebody whom I considered to be my friend. Within days the national Sunday papers were on to the story and, as if to remind me of the fact that I would never be able to lead a normal life again, once more what seemed like the whole world was prying into my private life.

In the event, there were two good things that came out of that particular blaze of publicity. The first was that it forced me to concentrate my mind on the subject of marriage to Omar.

Where would we live? Would his family reject me? What about his friends? If everyone in Omar's world refused to accept our relationship, wouldn't that make him resent me in time? The conclusion was staring me in the face. I must turn Omar's proposal down. When I broke the news to him he pleaded with me to change my mind, offering me every possible reassurance that he could. But I was adamant.

The second benefit was that it made me realize how genuine Steve's and James's friendship was. Until that moment I hadn't really been sure that they knew who I really was, so when the publicity broke I had begun to avoid them in the mistaken belief that they might not want to be associated with me. But they refused to let me to do this, telling me in no uncertain terms: 'When will you get it through your head that we love you for who you are – not *what* you are, or were.'

The absence of Omar's phone calls proved more painful than I had imagined, and many times I cried over what I thought could well have been my most disastrous mistake. With hindsight, I can see clearly now that my decision was right. Granted, I would have enjoyed incredible wealth and a fantastic lifestyle, but I doubt whether I would have found the same degree of happiness and contentment that I now have.

The time had come for me to give immediate consideration to my future. I knew I had to do something on my own, but what? I knew it had to be some venture in which my past and my background would not prove to be a major liability. Unfortunately, this ruled out most of the things I could think of. And even if I did come up with a suitable venture, what would I use for capital? I considered setting up a marketing consultancy business, but then the thought occurred to me that I might be boycotted by any reputable companies because of my notoriety.

It was whilst I was running through every possibility that I began to wonder where people like myself who were tall, or larger than 'normal' size, bought their clothes. This led me to pondering the problem of where transvestites – or TVs, as they are often known – got their female clothes, which in turn led to wondering about how many transvestites there might be in Britain. Researching this subject was far from easy, because by the very nature of their predilection transvestites do all they can to conceal this fact about themselves. But by visiting the local library, and through James's efforts to obtain specialist TV magazines for me, I was able to reach the conclusion that here was a market which was vastly under-catered to. Moreover, of those who were providing the means for TVs to indulge their relatively harmless hobby, the vast majority were exploiting the TVs' plight by selling shoddy goods at inflated prices in sleazy back street dives. The idea that started life as no more than idle wondering began to germinate, and before too long I had put together a complete proposal for a business that would cater exclusively to this market.

Percentage-wise the market couldn't possibly be that extensive; therefore, if the venture was to have any chance of succeeding, I would need access to densely populated areas. The northwest seemed to serve my needs well in that respect, and it also attracted a great deal of passing trade. When I looked at a map I saw that the easiest place to reach from north, south, east and west was Junction 17 on the M62.

My proposal included not just clothing, wigs, underwear and shoes, but absolutely everything a transvestite might conceivably need, including a beauty salon with trained staff to give advice on make-up, hair removal and every single piece of expertise that goes into making women beautiful. And as for the rest of the country beyond my reach – well, once the business was up and running, a confidential mail order service could easily reach the rest of the UK.

The only vital piece missing from my jigsaw was capital. Despite approaching numerous banks and finance companies, I reached the conclusion that the oft-repeated maxim was true: banks are only happy to lend you an umbrella on a sunny day. Without collateral I was stumped. No one was prepared to put up unsecured capital to finance such a venture, so there was only one avenue left for me to explore. I placed an advert in the *Manchester Evening News*: 'Mature businesswoman with innovative idea wishes to meet partner with capital in return for fifty per cent of the equity.' I received thirty-six replies. Some were immediately disqualified because of their tone, others after the first telephone conversation. I was now down to just eight which warranted a meeting.

One day over coffee I was telling Sandra, the beautician who had taught me so much about looking and behaving like a woman, of my plans. Suddenly she said: 'My brother Raiko's always fancied going into business'. She explained that Raiko was currently working for the British Shoe Corporation as a manager of one of their larger shops in Liverpool. A few days later I received a note through the post, asking me to ring Sandra urgently.

'I've mentioned the matter to my brother,' she said excitedly, 'and he's very interested in meeting you.' Sandra had an Italian mother and a Yugoslavian father; a nicer family one could never expect to meet, and Raiko, it soon transpired, was just as nice as everyone else. We clicked immediately and within twenty minutes we'd sealed a bargain to go into partnership, with Raiko investing every penny he had (£6000) in our joint venture.

The next step involved meeting the eight interested parties left on my list. Some were immediately put off as soon as they learned the nature of the business I intended to set up, while others I couldn't relate to and instinctively felt that a partnership would never work out. Only one of the eight, a woman, emerged as a front runner – until I made the mistake of inviting her round for a drink with James and Steve one night. Unfortunately, Steve had rather too much to drink and insisted on telling this lady her fortune, which apparently consisted mainly of 'dark waters'. Whether it was Steve's dire predictions or something else that put her off I'll never know, but in the event I received a negative response from her two days later.

All I had left now was one last note which I had initially disregarded on the basis that it was scribbled on the letter heading of a company called Booth and Booth, who described themselves as 'suppliers of food to Lancashire and Cheshire'. The company sounded grand enough, but it was the very brief message and the almost illegible scrawl that worried me, for it merely said 'Ring ...' followed by a telephone number and a signature that was virtually indecipherable. But what did I have to lose? After all, there weren't any other runners left in the race now. In a far from optimistic mood I rang the number and spoke to Mr Booth, who arranged to visit me to discuss my proposition. Many months later I learned that it was literally only as he was setting off to meet me that David Booth discovered my identity from an item in the evening paper. Thank goodness David was not the kind of man who chooses to judge a book by its cover!

Promptly at eight David arrived and, after being invited in, immediately took off his jacket, rolled up his sleeves and proceeded to make himself at home. Over coffee I explained that, with Raiko financing the retail side, I still needed capital for the mail order operation and beauty salon. David's response to my outline ideas was fairly non-committal: he only said that it would be essential for me to meet his wife, who was in partnership with him.

Meanwhile, Raiko and I were busy trying to find the right

premises in the location that I had pin-pointed, as well as suitable suppliers – the latter proved to be far more difficult than either of us had envisaged. On Raiko's one day off each week we would scour the locality visiting potential suppliers and inspecting premises. We must have made a very odd couple indeed, with me touching six feet in height and Raiko barely five feet four, but never once did Raiko give me any reason to imagine that he was either embarrassed to be seen with me or had any hang-ups about our relationship.

We eventually found a suitable property which, despite being fairly run down, met with most of our criteria. The fact that it had been reduced from £40,000 to £35,000 also helped make it more appealing. I approached the local shopkeepers' agency, who arranged to have the property surveyed on our behalf; they recommended that we didn't go above £30,000. To undercut the original asking price by £5000 when it had already been reduced by the same amount seemed a bit risky to me, but we did as we were advised. The plan was that the shopkeepers' agency would buy the property and then lease it to us at £6000 per annum over a period of six years.

At that point Bob intervened, offering to buy the property outright and rent it to us on the same terms as the shopkeepers' agency were offering. I was undecided. On the one hand I didn't really want anyone interfering in our business; on the other, Bob and I were still good friends. Eventually, Bob said that if I rented the property from him he'd leave it to me in his will. I was surprised for once by his generosity. In the meantime, we could have it on a nine-year lease with an option to buy the freehold after six.

At the same time as these negotiations were taking place, my period of tenancy at the house in West Houghton was up. The obvious solution was to live in the flat above the shop, and that's precisely what I did. I moved into the flat on 5 July 1984, much to the consternation of the local Prestwich residents who were horrified to have such a notorious person as an immediate neighbour. A further three months were to elapse before we took possession of the shop premises, but what with the flat, a jungle of a garden to transform, stock to buy and a myriad of other details to sort out before we would finally be ready to do business, I had plenty to keep me occupied.

In the meantime David Booth had arranged for me to meet his wife, Ethel over a drink. Ethel, it transpired, had been virtually blind with acute myopia when David and she had first met. Because this condition is very much linked to the state of the nerves, her ability to see would vary, though her sight was never particularly good and she relied very much on a guide dog to help her get around.

The meeting went well, despite the fact (as I later learned) that Ethel was extremely nervous about meeting someone as infamous as me. A few days later David telephoned to say that, having been in the retail food business for fifteen years, he and Ethel had decided it was now time to expand their interests and take a chance on something different. Having been impressed with my proposals and my professional background, they both felt their money would be wisely invested in me. We decided to form several companies under the banner name of Transformation, with me as a 50 per cent shareholder and either Raiko or David holding the other 50 per cent according to the interests of the particular company.

As so often happens, when things begin to sort themselves out in one area of your life, you find that everything else starts improving, too. I had been far too preoccupied with the launch of Transformation to give much thought to a social life, so when I received an invitation for drinks at the house of an acquaintance one evening I didn't feel particularly inclined to accept. In the event, I was ridiculously pleased that I had agreed to go, for it was there that I met Peter and fell head over heels in love for the first time as a woman.

At just twenty-eight Peter was not only ten years younger than I, but incredibly good-looking too. From the moment we were introduced he made it quite plain that he was interested in me, and I was immensely flattered. As we talked and relaxed in each other's company, I learned that he was only visiting Manchester for the weekend to attend a local authority conference and that he actually lived and worked in the north-east. Peter was so charming and attractive, and so obviously attracted to me, that I was hooked. By the end of the evening I felt like a starry-eyed teenager in love for the first time in her life, and when he offered to come down the following weekend just to see me I agreed immediately.

Ours was a whirlwind romance and, like most such lightning affairs, it was exceedingly intense with ridiculously high peaks and painfully low troughs. We couldn't wait to be with each other at weekends, and during the week we would spend hours talking on the telephone. I was so infatuated that the only person who couldn't see the potential danger was me.

Each weekend, for forty-eight passionate, romantic hours nothing could separate us; when we weren't in bed, Peter would be right alongside me helping to paint the walls in the shop or putting up shelves – anything, so long as he could be with me. Within a very short time he was like one of the family and both David and Raiko accepted his presence in my life (and, consequently, in theirs) without comment.

Privately, however, Raiko had his doubts. Though he kept them to himself at the time, I later learned that he had always felt Peter was far too unambitious for me and leaned on me far more than was good for either of us. But I was so besotted with Peter that when he began to talk about finding a job in Manchester and of getting married I was too overjoyed and excited to worry about the fact that it was all happening much too soon. When I was with him at the weekends, my mind was full of him and the wonderful future we would have together, and when we were apart during the week I filled my thoughts with plans for Transformation.

On 13 October we were finally ready to open. The *Manchester Evening News* had published a photograph of me standing outside the shop holding a notice declaring that we would be 'opening shortly', and our first week's business was encouraging. Obviously the female population thought we were a straightforward beauty salon providing all the services that beauty salons provide, while the closet TV population of the area knew from our discreet ads in the *Manchester Evening News* and TV press that here was a local business that could provide for all their needs.

However, as one might expect, this mix of clientele was not without its problematical (and hysterical) moments. We'd hired two young assistants, Maria and Karen, to help out in the shop so that Raiko could continue working at his day job, and quite often I'd be in the difficult position of having a woman in one cubicle having her legs waxed with a man in the next secretly having the same treatment!

We worked long hours, opening seven days a week till ten every night, but it wasn't enough to make the business a success. Even with our stringent budgetary controls and a hastily arranged overdraft it didn't take long to realize that we were struggling to keep afloat. As a trainee accountant, Peter proved very useful when it came to doing the books for us each weekend, but there was no hiding from the truth: we were heading for financial disaster.

David took no part in the day-to-day running of the business because he had his supermarket chain to take care of. Besides, he trusted Raiko and myself to get on with the business of Transformation, and didn't see any need for anything more than a weekly update. Raiko and I began to feel depressed and concerned, and soon even Peter's weekly visits, welcome as they were, weren't enought to lift my spirits.

By the time Christmas approached I was beginning to despair: if business didn't perk up soon, I'd be in the unhappy position of being responsible for letting down the only two people in the world who had had sufficient belief in me to invest their hard-earned money in my plans. And as if things weren't looking bleak enough, during one of Peter's weekend visits I realized that something else was obviously going wrong. His attitude was different, and though it was only a subtle change I began to fear the worst. By the Saturday my fears were confirmed: Peter wanted to finish our affair.

I was heartbroken. My first true boyfriend, who just a few weeks previously had been discussing wedding plans, was now telling me he no longer wanted me. The pain was indescribable. Peter had to stay with me all weekend because he had dropped his brother off in Leeds and wasn't able to collect him until Sunday. It must have been terrible for him; all I could do was mope around with tears streaming down my cheeks, begging him to tell me the reason why. He never did say, but I assume it had something to do with my background.

When he walked out of my life that Sunday afternoon I was devastated. Once again I knew what it was like to be alone. If it hadn't been for Raiko's tremendous support, and the fact that I now had a business to bury myself in, I don't know how I would have coped. I was in such an emotional state that for the first five days I could hardly bring myself to get out of bed. All I could do was cry my heart out, alternating between dementedly ranting at fate and bitterly declaring that I now hated all men. Raiko tried his hardest to cheer me up, but he was fighting a losing battle. I could not sleep, eat nor summon any interest in work. As a weight loss programme I knew no equal. Physically, mentally and emotionally I was in such a hopeless mess that I felt the best thing I could do would be to leave both the flat and the business and start all over again. Fortunately, David and Raiko were both marvellously supportive and refused even to consider such a prospect.

On the sixth day I finally managed to pull myself together.

Telling myself that it was only my ego and my pride that had been dented, I conceived a plan which was specifically designed to salvage both, while at the same wreaking some form of revenge on Peter for hurting me so badly. I telephoned Peter and asked him to stop by when he came to Manchester for an interview the following week.

'Do you think that's wise?' he said.

'Don't be silly,' I protested. 'After all, there's no reason why we can't still be friends.'

'All right, then,' Peter agreed, somewhat doubtfully.

Having got Peter to see me, I smiled to myself as I put the phone down. I wanted to make Peter realize what he had lost and could never have back again.

The following weekend I dressed to kill. I selected the sexiest, slinkiest outfit and the most tantalizing underwear and highest heels I possessed. I took hours over my make-up and sprayed on the most expensive perfume I owned. Confident that I looked both stunning and seductive, I had absolutely no doubts about my ability to be so provocative and alluring that Peter couldn't help but be putty in my hands.

When he arrived I was polite and distant, keeping him at arm's length. I could see he was confused, and I knew that my behaviour was childish, to say the least, but I also knew that survival was the name of the game. If I could make Peter want me again it would go some way towards healing my bruised ego. And if I could have the satisfaction of being the one to do the rejecting this time, then perhaps my dignity, pride and belief in myself might once again be restored.

Poor Peter – he didn't stand a chance. I flirted and teased outrageously until he was so turned on that all he could think about was dragging me off to bed. And then I said no. My behaviour was cruel and unkind, but the end justified the means, for my ploy worked and for the first time I had no doubts about my ability to survive this latest blow.

If only all our problems could have been dealt with so easily! With each passing week Transformation was doing less business. In an attempt to cut costs Raiko left his job and joined me full time so that we could manage without staff. We paid ourselves only £30 a week, yet despite every economy we would be facing bankruptcy if things didn't pick up soon. But when things are at their darkest, salvation often comes along in the strangest of forms and works in the most mysterious of ways.

9
UNUSUAL SERVICES

With the loss of our trained beautician the only person left to do the salon treatments was me; I'd had no formal training, but had been practising long enough to feel competent. One of our regular customers was a lady called Yvonne, whom I'd become fairly friendly with in a business-like way. When Yvonne casually asked one day how the business was doing, I told her how difficult we were finding things and confided my fears for the future.

'What you need, Stephanie, is a new service.'

'What do you mean?' I asked.

'Well, perhaps you should consider offering a massage service for gentlemen,' she suggested bluntly.

I couldn't even begin to imagine what Yvonne was trying to say. 'What do you mean? For gentlemen?'

'You know, with "extras" provided on the side. It would help to get you out of the financial mess you're in. And besides, it's perfectly legal if you do it in the right way.'

I was so taken aback by Yvonne's suggestion and the casual way she had mentioned it that I didn't begin to consider it seriously, particularly as I was certain it couldn't be legal. However, when she next visited the salon and repeated her idea, I began to wonder.

'Look,' she insisted. 'It really *is* legal if it's only a single girl. If you don't believe me, why not give my solicitor a call? He'll certainly back up what I'm telling you.'

I still couldn't take Yvonne's suggestion seriously – though I mentioned it in passing to Raiko, who agreed with me that it sounded highly illegal. A few weeks later Yvonne appeared in the salon again and asked whether I had spoken to her solicitor, Geoff, yet. Exasperated when I confessed I hadn't, Yvonne took matters into her own hands and arranged an appointment.

Raiko and I were by this time so worried about business that we decided we had nothing to lose by checking Yvonne's story out, so I went along to Geoff's impressive office in Manchester to hear what he had to say. Geoff turned out to be a highly

intelligent and very successful solicitor who specialized in handling some of the more newsworthy criminal cases. He was very
friendly, very personable and quite obviously very much a
ladies' man, and when I told him of the reason for my visit he
assured me that there was nothing in the law that prevented a
girl from offering sexual favours to clients for reward, providing
that she worked entirely on her own.

I returned home in a thoughtful mood, conscious of the fact
that I would have preferred it if Geoff hadn't confirmed what
Yvonne had said, because now I was presented with a dilemma
that I had no real wish to face. Even if it was legal, could I really
cope with doing such a thing? And if I could, was I capable of
offering the kind of services that Yvonne had suggested?

I recounted everything to an incredulous Raiko. As I wanted
him to hear the facts from Geoff himself, I arranged for us to visit
him together, and this time we went along armed with a list of
questions. Once again Geoff assured us that, providing we stuck
to the rules of just one girl working alone, I couldn't possibly be
accused of doing anything outside the law. Raiko and I spent
many hours trying on the idea for size, but before we were ready
to give it further consideration we felt it would be wise to invite
Geoff along to the shop to check out the premises. Raiko also felt
that, as it was such a drastic step to take, it was a decision that
only I could make.

In the event, the decision was taken right out of my hands.
For when Geoff arrived the following evening, after giving his
seal of approval to our premises, he astounded us both with a
suggestion all of his own: that he should become my first
customer! I didn't even have time to digest what he had said
before I found myself being taken upstairs, and then demon-
strating what was soon to become part of a familiar repertoire of
providing oral sex and full sex in return for monetary gain.

When it was over, a clearly well-satisfied Geoff turned to me
and said: 'Now, how much do I owe you?'

Caught off guard, highly embarrassed and unnerved by this
matter-of-fact transaction, I flustered: 'Well, I'm not sure ... I
mean ... hell, why don't you just pay me what it was worth?'

Fifty pounds poorer, Geoff then left Raiko and me alone to
discuss this amazing piece of providence. Both of us were
amazed by the whole thing, and even more so by the fact that I
had been able to handle the whole thing with emotional detach-
ment. If £50 was the going rate, we thought, it wouldn't take us
very long to get our business back on to its feet!

Emboldened by the exercise – and by the fifty crisp notes now filling our empty till – Raiko and I immediately went to a wholesaler's where we purchased a gross of condoms. Then we placed an advertisement in the personal column of the *Manchester Evening News*, which read: 'Massage and all facilities provided by attractive transsexual.' Can anyone believe how naïve we were?

The phone calls began to pour in and, delighted but undoubtedly green as grass, we answered every call openly and honestly. I must confess it makes me go hot and cold to think of it now, but we were so innocent and believed so totally in what Geoff had told us that we felt absolutely relaxed about being completely frank on the telephone. If a prospective customer asked what services were available, we would list everything we could think of from hand relief to oral sex; bondage to domination; and just about every other conceivable sexual need that came to mind.

Of course, neither of us was naïve enough to inform David about what was going on. We both sensed that he would not only wholeheartedly disapprove, but would almost certainly raise every objection that he could. And so it was that I embarked on a new career which, in addition to saving Transformation, also provided some of the most enlightening and often hysterically humorous episodes of my entire career.

Our decision had been made so suddenly that we weren't properly equipped to handle all the demands that our new services created. We had a massage couch, of course, because that was an integral piece of equipment for the salon, but apart from that we could only learn what was required as we went along. Thus the first customers who responded to our advertisements were very often closeted in a cubicle right next to another which was occupied by a woman undergoing a conventional (and, as it turned out, more legal) form of treatment.

I soon learned to develop a loud, hasty cough to cover the potentially embarrassing noises that a client might make at certain 'sensitive' moments. We even installed a radio and started playing loud music to cover up the often unmistakable sounds of mounting sexual excitement that would emanate from behind the curtains. However, it took a while for me to come up with an alternative arrangement that would deal with the problem of a gentleman's uncontrollably twitching feet sticking out through the curtains of a cubicle which had been designed with a whole range of other purposes in mind! Soon, playing this cat and mouse game of trying to prevent one side of the business from interfering with the more legitimate side was beginning to tax even Raiko's and my own far from limited ingenuity.

Still, we were taking more money than we'd seen in months, and very often we'd earn more in one day than we'd previously earned in an entire week! But Raiko and I still only took the same wage of £30 a week, because we wanted to plough all the money straight back into the business in order to get the company out of trouble as quickly as we possibly could.

However, it soon became obvious that we couldn't possibly continue to run the service in this way without causing major disruptions to the rest of the salon, so we carried the massage couch upstairs into the flat, which gave me more room and made Raiko's life downstairs a little less fraught. We bought a couple of chairs, a little table and a few bottles of spirits and put these at the bottom of the stairs so that clients could have free drinks and a magazine to read while they waited their turn. And, of course, with a bathroom and shower upstairs in the flat the problems of hygiene could also now be taken care of in a more discreet and thorough manner.

Gradually, and by word of mouth my 'fame' was beginning to spread. Once again we were able to employ staff to run the salon downstairs under Raiko's eagle eye, while I was by now fully occupied upstairs earning the money to support our venture. With our more pressing financial problems easing, I was able to feel a certain sense of pride in my new 'business'. Therefore, if I had a client with specific needs that were difficult to satisfy I would often apply my marketing brain to devise a solution that was guaranteed to meet their objectives.

David was still blithely ignorant of the true nature of our new 'business success'. When he innocently enquired, during one weekly visit, why I had a massage couch in the middle of my lounge, I convinced him that, as we were now so popular with the ladies, we'd decided to invest in a second couch (for which there was no room downstairs) rather than lose out on potential business!

Human nature being as curious as it is, I'm sure many readers will be amused by some of the stranger (and more amusing) people and requests that became an everyday part of my life.

One of my first regular clients was a man whom we nick-named Mr Blackburn, after the town from which he came. Mr B was a stoutly built individual who took to coming in late on Saturday evenings. During our first encounter he shyly told me that he was totally unable to enjoy 'normal' sex and was very much addicted to pain, complaining that no girl he had ever visited had been able to provide sufficient pain for him to experience complete pleasure and satisfaction.

Far from being shocked, I was able to sympathise with Mr B's unfortunate plight. Armed with padlocks, whips and lengths of chain, I soon had him helplessly trussed like a chicken on the couch as I deployed my entire repertoire of domination techniques in order to provide him with the relief he so desperately sought. I tried a schoolroom cane first, discarding it in favour of a cat o' nine tails when it obviously proved inadequate. Unfortunately Mr B proved to be a tough customer in more ways than one, and at the end of his allotted time I was still no nearer to finding an effective solution to his problem because there were several impatient clients waiting for their turn.

'Look, don't worry about this. Come back next week and I promise you I'll do my utmost to come up with something that will work for you,' I promised the crestfallen Mr B as he departed down the stairs with a disappointed, hangdog expression on his chubby face. And I meant it! After all, my entire career success had been founded on the premise that if a job's worth doing, it's worth doing well. And just because I'd changed my career path, I didn't feel that was any reason to change my business methods. So it was that during the next week I spent all my spare time wrestling with the problem of how to satisfy poor Mr B's particular needs – without causing the man any permanent damage, that is!

By the time he arrived for his next appointment, at the same time the following week, I was convinced I had come up with an idea that would produce the desired effect. Once again I shackled and bound him to the couch, this time face upwards. Then I proceeded to apply my brand-new state-of-the-art equipment – a dozen wooden clothes pegs! – which I attached to his ears, nipples and testicles. Now the amazing thing about clothes pegs is that, while they don't actually hurt when you pinch them on to skin, they do effectively cut off the circulation to the parts of the body to which they are applied – and if you leave them on long enough, when they're removed the pain caused by the free flow of blood and return of feeling to the affected parts is excruciating.

Poor Mr B's face when he saw that my equipment consisted of nothing more than a set of clothes pegs was the most graphic picture of thwarted hopes I have ever seen. However I had another secret weapon up my sleeve! I lit a candle and dripped molten wax on to Mr B's exposed thighs, trailing a deliberately slow line upwards in the direction of his private parts.

'Ha!' I thought to myself. 'That certainly ought to do the trick,' as I watched his panic-stricken face when it dawned on him just what I had in mind. The look of terror in his fear-maddened eyes grew in direct proportion to the size of the previously inert penis that was now suddenly springing into joyful life. Responding to my enquiring look, Mr B. signalled that I should go on – at which point I was delighted to oblige, confident that this time I'd cracked what was, for him, a very difficult problem and finally bring him to the peak of fulfilment. Alas, I was wrong.

'Next week, I promise you,' I said consolingly as I shepherded the forlorn man out of the door, though truth to tell I hadn't a clue what I could possibly dream up that might satisfy this one.

Once again I spent an entire week's free time thinking around and around Mr B's problem, and it was only when he was finally due to appear again that I had a sudden flash of inspiration. Without any time for lengthy experimentation, I moved the necessary salon equipment upstairs to my lounge. When he arrived, with a pathetically hopeful look on his face, I was able this time to promise an unqualified success.

We went through the now familiar ritual of trussing him up like a fowl, but on this occasion I added the further innovation of gagging him with a dildo in order to heighten his sexual tension. As I uncovered my masterstroke before his disbelieving eyes and plugged the apparatus into the mains, the sheer terror on his face caused me to wonder whether it was possible for a human being to die either from the shock or the ecstasy. Momentarily I wondered whether I was doing the right thing, but fortunately Mr B's fervently nodding head assured me that I was.

The equipment I had selected consisted of a sophisticated beauty treatment machine. Two glass rods were connected via thick leads to a unit which produced high-frequency galvanic and faradic impulses. When applied to the face for specific beauty treatments, the glass bulbs conducted an electrical charge into the lower levels of the skin in order to stimulate blood flow to its surface. Although this procedure can prove painful, most women swear the discomfort is worth it for the remarkable effects it has on skin tone.

Placing the glass half an inch away from Mr B's nipples, I adjusted the controls to increase the output (and therefore, the amount of pain I would be inflicting) while at the same time keeping a watchful eye on his face in case he should decide that enough was far too much for him! Slowly I moved towards the organ that persistently refused to provide the satisfaction he so obviously craved. As the electrical charge shot through Mr B's nether parts the results were even more spectacular and rewarding than either of us had hoped. Within seconds Mr B's head was nodding an ever-increasing frantic dance of encouragement until finally (and thankfully) he gave a strangled yelp as the desired effect was achieved.

Mr B was so pathetically grateful that he couldn't thank me enough. He insisted on paying me twice the normal fee, and within a few days I was inundated with deliveries of champagne and chocolates. As for myself? Well, it was most gratifying to learn that at least there was one person in the world who was happy to have known me.

Then there was the strange man who always insisted on leaving his shoes and socks on while I gave him his 'massage'. Now, frankly, like most people I've always thought there is no sight more ludicrous than a man naked but for his socks and shoes. Still, if that was what the customer wanted, who was I to disagree? However, what really surprised me about this gent was that, when I went into the bathroom to chat with him for a while after one appointment, I saw him standing in the shower stall beneath a cascade of steaming water *still wearing those ubiquitous socks and shoes*! When he left the flat and squelched down the stairs I could barely control my shaking shoulders.

Another customer became known as 'The Wrestler' because he always wanted me to cover myself and him with baby oil and spend fifteen minutes wrestling all over the floor with me. Naturally (and naïvely, as it transpired) I assumed that we would merely play at wrestling. Not so, for 'The Wrestler' really meant business. Fortunately for me, oil makes the skin extremely slippery. So despite the fact that 'The Wrestler' did manage to get a good enough grip to throw me around a bit, he never quite managed to do any real damage – because he'd always get so excited he'd have to have sex with me on the floor right there and then.

One incident taught me that the difference between a hero and a heel is just a matter of perception. A customer came to call, enjoyed both oral and full sex, and then sat chatting to me for the remainder of his allotted time before leaving. Imagine my surprise when the next day I opened up the *Manchester Evening News* to find this customer being hailed as a hero because, having arrived home the day before to find his wife in the very last stages of labour, he'd single-handedly delivered his own child before the ambulance crew arrived. I wonder what that same wife (or the press, for that matter) would have had to say had they known where he'd spent the afternoon.

After some weeks of offering this new service, I was becoming quite blasé about the variety of odd predilections that my customers invariably seemed to favour. However, there were still one or two surprises in store for me. One day a new customer arrived for his appointment with a very strange request. Although I was momentarily nonplussed, I soon recovered my composure enough to rush down the stairs to the salon and say to Raiko, 'Quick, run down to the stationers and bring me back the largest cardboard box you can possibly find, together with lots of brown paper, sellotape and string.'

Raiko's face was a picture. 'What on earth do you want a large box, paper, sellotape and string for? This is hardly the time or place to start practising origami!'

'Don't ask questions now – just go and get it!' I hissed in return.

Poor Raiko did as he was told, but he could hardly contain his curiosity. The moment the customer had left he ran up the stairs two at a time to find me collapsed in fits of laughter on the bed.

'What did he want?' he asked as I lay there giggling and saying, 'That was the easiest fifty pounds I've ever earned.'

Eventually I calmed down enough to tell him what had transpired. When a more than bemused Raiko had returned with the 'equipment', my customer stripped his clothes off, climbed into the box and then bade me seal it up with sellotape, then wrap the brown paper around it, secure it with more sellotape and finally tie it up with string. After that was done I had to go through the whole process in reverse, with the strict instruction to jump back in feigned surprise as soon as my 'jack in the box' was revealed. This, apparently, was all it took to stimulate the poor man to climax.

Then there was the man we christened 'Humpty Dumpty' because of his obsession with eggs. When he first appeared for his appointment you could have knocked me down with a feather when in reply to my usual question: 'Is there any other service you require, sir?' he said, 'Yes. Do you have a dozen eggs?'

Surely he can't want me to cook an omelette? I thought to myself. I went into the kitchen, looked in the fridge and saw that we were right out of eggs. So, quick as a flash, I raced downstairs and hissed at Raiko: 'Nip round the corner and bring back a dozen eggs.' Fortunately, by that time Raiko was more than used to me running downstairs with all kinds of strange requests, and had long since learned to restrain himself from asking awkward questions until after the customers had all gone, when we would relax and have a little laugh about the day's odd events. Anyhow, Raiko returned with two cartons of eggs which he slapped into my hands with a smile, and back upstairs I went.

'I've got the eggs,' I said to the customer.

'Well, then, perhaps we ought to go into the bathroom.'

I was dying to discover what exactly he wanted to do with the eggs but managed to control my curiosity and wait until he was ready to show me. Once we were in the bathroom he asked me to dress him in a pair of my knickers and then carefully place the dozen eggs inside the knickers. Then I had to slap my hands against the eggs so that the shells would break and the gooey mixture would run down his thighs and legs – and that was it! When the recent eggs and salmonella scare was filling the newspapers, I did wonder whether Humpty Dumpty might have given up his little hobby for fear of catching the disease!

One other inexplicable oddity was the man who liked to have gooey cream cakes thrown at him so that the light sponge and cream would stick to his body. He used to remind me of a dartboard. The only problem was that, as I've never had a particularly good aim, the cakes and cream would end up all over the place. Heaven knows what Karen used to think when I calmly went downstairs and asked her to clean up the bathroom as there were 'a load of cream cakes all over the floor'.

Naturally, not all my clients were odd. Some were quite ordinary and only required the 'normal' service of straight sex. On the other hand, some were far from 'ordinary' and still required no more than straight sex!

One such young man was a very famous singer and actor, and no one was more surprised than me when he showed up for his appointment. To my relief, he didn't require anything extraordinary (which I'm sure would have shattered mine and a million other women's illusions about this gorgeous hunk of masculinity if he had), and throughout the session neither of us made any reference to his celebrity. Thus I was able to treat him just the same as any other customer. Sad to say, his 'performance' off stage and in my bed was pretty ordinary, too, despite the fact that I made one small concession and gave him an extra five minutes for his money. Still, he did move me to do one out-of-the-ordinary thing: I went out and bought his record, which was in the top ten at the time.

Some fetishes that most people find hard to understand are, in reality, fairly common. For example, there are many men with shoe or feet fetishes, and I'm sure every prostitute has come across at least one of these in her time. I had one customer who was a 'shoe' man, and all he required was that I make an extremely slow and sensuous display of smoothing on a pair of stockings, raising my skirt and fastening them to my suspenders, and then sliding my feet into a pair of preposterously high stiletto heels. I merely had to walk around for a few minutes before, equally slowly, reversing the process. I didn't need to undress or remove any other article of clothing, nor did I have to touch him or perform any other service, for throughout the whole performance my client would sit across the other side of the room and masturbate himself to orgasm. That was enough for him – and, of course, it was more than all right with me.

One famous personality appearing in a Manchester show turned up on my doorstep, followed by several judges, police-men and VIPs. Within months news of my services had spread fast. The story went around that not only was I unique, but I was committed to providing total satisfaction *and* I was also remarkably discreet.

Now that I have become well-known, I am always being asked by the Sunday papers to reveal all the private details of my long list of clients. In fact, one national editor once remarked: 'If Christine Keeler could bring Profumo down and Sara Keays could do the same for Cecil Parkinson, with what you know, Stephanie, you could probably single-handedly bring the entire government to its knees!' My response then was the same as it is now: I just give an enigmatic smile and shrug my shoulders. Only I, Raiko and now David know what dynamite my unexpurgated memoirs would really be – but I've taken a vow of confidentiality towards all my past personal clients, which extends to every customer who uses my mail order service or ventures into any of my shops. Should my vow of confiden-tiality need any explanation, it becomes obvious when I tell you that a large proportion of my more famous clients were (and probably still are) into kinky sex.

One VIP whom I shall refer to as Frank spent his entire hour with me as happy as a sandboy because I allowed him to clean my oven and toilet clad only in stockings, suspenders and a little maid's cap, with me scolding and berating him for being a naughty boy. That hour always culminated in the same scenario, in which I'd have to spank him for not doing his jobs properly.

Then there was the politician who liked me to dress him up in outsize baby clothes, spoon-feed him with tinned baby food and then allow him to lie curled up in the foetal position suckling a full bottle of milk! I'm sorely tempted to say that perhaps the bottle was a poor substitute for feeding at his leader's breast, but as his leader is now male such a comment could be misconstrued! Yet another politician wanted to be suspended by a chain wrapped around his testicles so that he was forced to stand on extreme tippy-toe, while all I had to do was return to him every fifteen minutes and whip his buttocks.

There were, of course, many others who adored being chained, spanked or dressed in one humiliating fashion or another – and all of these were overjoyed if I allowed them to paint my flat, dig my garden, act as my footstool or be my slave and lick my feet and shoes. In fact, the more important they were, the more desperately they seemed to crave domination and humiliation.

Before too long most of our regular customers had nicknames like those I've already mentioned. One rule we made was that we never asked a customer to supply his real name, and I never asked any leading questions that might possibly identify who they were or what they did. Sometimes I would have been hard pushed even to recognize them if I saw them out in the street. Yet on more than one occasion after business, when Raiko and I popped out for a meal at a local restaurant, we couldn't help but become aware of a table full of men (or a man who might be out for a meal with his wife or girlfriend) suddenly start shifting uncomfortably in their seats, or even change seats so their backs were to me. One highly embarrassed customer even went so far as to dive beneath the table to avoid being recognized by me! He really shouldn't have bothered, because invariably Raiko would turn to me and say: 'Do you recognize that man who's trying to pretend not to see you?'

And I'd reply: 'No. Should I?'

'You ought to,' Raiko would say, 'he was in last night . . . and him in that corner . . . and those guys over there have been in on several occasions.'

Without doubt, the most bizarre encounter of my career occurred when Raiko ushered in a new customer one day. I took one look at the man's eminently recognizable face and nearly fainted with shock. What compounded my surprise was the fact that, apart from being a very important cabinet minister, he and I had actually met before! Years before, when Marylin and I were still living together, she had been working part-time for the local Tory Party agent. One night we attended a function in honour of a well-known politician who had recently been embroiled in a scandal. Curious to meet the man face to face, I had been introduced. We'd shook hands and then spent several minutes exchanging small talk.

Now here he was in my flat, eager to part with £50 for my services – and, by all accounts, totally unaware of the fact that we had already met *when I had been a man*! Needless to say, like the consummate professional I prided myself on being, I swiftly managed to overcome my surprise and get on with the business at hand. But I must confess to having to stifle a secret chuckle at the thought of his reaction were I to remind him of the circumstances in which we had met before – somehow I don't think he would have been too pleased!

Every prostitute who has ever gone on record about her profession has likened herself to being a combination of whore, sister, mother, agony aunt and social worker – and I guess I feel just the same, for it gave me great pleasure to be able to solve people's problems for them. One young man in particular I remember well because he was so desperately shy and so badly wanted to lose his virginity. He was just nineteen and a poor foreign student, and though in an attempt to solve his problem we went beyond the hour he had paid for, it gave me immense satisfaction finally to bring this lad to fulfilment and to know that because of me he will never again be terrified of having sex with a woman.

I lost track of the sheer numbers of men who wanted to don female underwear or babywear, or be tied up and spanked, and over the months I began to understand why prostitutes are so much in demand when regular girlfriends and wives are so reluctant to do anything outside the 'norm'. Certainly the majority of my customers were outwardly happily married men, but the very fact that they needed to indulge their more secret fantasies only with me often made me wonder how *happily* married they might really be were it their wives who were catering for their special needs out of love rather than a hooker who did it for cash.

Without doubt prostitution is a very difficult profession, and to all those who think it consists of nothing more than lying there examining cracks in the ceiling or mentally compiling shopping lists while a series of men hand over lots of money in return for little effort, all I can say is: you couldn't be more misinformed. We were open seven days a week from eleven in the morning till eleven at night, and I was on the go the entire time. Regular meals were strangers to me, and with a continuous circle of clients arriving and leaving there was little time even for the fastest of 'fast foods'. I rarely left the flat apart from our once-a-week shopping trip at Sainsbury's. Now I dread to think of what people must have thought as Raiko and I rushed around the aisles throwing food into our trolley, with me dressed in the highest of heels, the micro-est of mini-skirts (time was in such short supply that I had to dress for 'work' before we went to the supermarket) and the flimsiest of tops, with a coat hastily thrown on over this bizarre ensemble.

Business was booming, and to help cope with the increasing number of telephone calls we received we hired a nice young Jewish girl to handle the calls and book appointments. Despite the odd nature of our business she applied herself as assiduously to her duties as if she were working for the local dentist, and was soon providing verbal details of the services on offer over the phone and assisting transvestites in the shop without so much as batting an eyelid.

Raiko, being a natural-born wheeler-dealer, soon became adept at bartering my services and obtaining many bargains too. Many's the time he'd show a new client up the stairs and slip me a note saying something like 'This one's a freebie – we're getting a new carpet for the salon', and I'd just as often pass back a note which said something incredibly boring and normal like 'Don't forget to defrost the prawns for supper!' before disappearing into my lounge or bedroom to perform my latest exotic party trick.

Ultimately, of course, things couldn't possibly go on as they were; through outside interference, the Happy Hooker episode in my life came to an abrupt end. But before I relate how that came about, let me forestall the inevitable question: 'How on earth could you bring yourself to do all those degrading things?' with this explanation.

The answer is, under normal circumstances I wouldn't have had to. Unfortunately, necessity is a very powerful motivater indeed. If you doubt that, just think about the survivors of plane crashes who have had to resort to cannibalism in order to stay alive. In my case, if I had been the only person involved in the

Transformation business, nothing would have induced me to go to such lengths to save it. But as it was, to lose the money of the only two people in the world who had shown such personal faith and trust in me was, to my mind, a far worse alternative than prostitution. (Besides, let's not forget that I had been assured on very good authority that what I was doing was legal.) I owed everything to David and Raiko, and given the same circumstances all over again I would take precisely the same action.

The second thing I have to say about what I did may surprise some people. I didn't find it at all difficult to cater to those unfortunate men's needs, because I never allowed what was happening physically to affect me emotionally or mentally. Kissing (which I believe is far more intimate and personal than anything I might ever have done with other parts of my body) was strictly taboo, as was touching my hair, fondling my face or any other kind of contact above the neck. I could use my mouth and lips to perform oral sex on my clients only because that was a necessary part of the service and because I remained in control – not them. By remaining in control mentally, I was able to train myself to live outside my body during moments of physical intimacy. Every prostitute will tell you that every client wants to believe he is the very best – which is why prostitutes are experts when it comes to faking orgasm. Even when I appeared to be in the throes of the noisiest and most earth-shattering orgasm any man could ever dream of giving a woman, my brain was always totally disconnected.

But mentally distanced or not, this part of my career soon came to an end. Early one afternoon I was in the early stages of massaging a client who had already paid me for full sex. My client was lying face down on his stomach while I was standing beside him, stark naked, massaging his back and shoulders. Suddenly we were interrupted by three men who crashed through the door. My first thought was to wonder what on earth Raiko must be thinking of to send three men up at once.

'Is your name Stephanie Anne Lloyd?' one of the men asked as he flashed his warrant card.

Dumbly I nodded.

'You are not obliged to say anything, but anything you do say will be taken down and may be given in evidence.' All I could see was this poor man, who had just parted with his money for a little bit of heaven, now clinging ashen-faced to both his dignity and the couch and feeling like hell.

'Do you think I could be allowed to get dressed?' I enquired politely. One of the detectives nodded and so I went into the bedroom – closely followed, I might add, by the other two, who stood and watched me with undisguised interest while I put on my underwear and a dress before they escorted me out of the shop and into a waiting unmarked car.

I later learned that the raid had been sparked off by a complaint from a neighbour who, it transpired, had been busily employed in spying on me for several months. Apparently, by having stupidly placed a large mirror on the wall directly opposite the upstairs window, I had unwittingly nullified the effect of the net curtain at the windows and offered this fortunate man a totally uninterrupted view of everything that was going on in my living room. Why this outraged member of the local community didn't simply come across and complain to us personally I shall never understand – or why it had taken him so long to report us, either! Suffice it to say that, whatever his motives, he did finally make a complaint and the police, bless them, responded in a style that would have justified the kind of operation put into effect following the Great Train Robbery. Rooms in the house opposite had been commandeered to allow visual observation; plain clothes officers were sent in with radio receivers and microphones wired up for sound; and the whole exercise was conducted with all the fanfare – and the same amount of comical bungling – as a Keystone Kops film. For, as I later found out, by sheer coincidence a young rep on her first working day for L'Amor cosmetics had arrived just before the police with her area manager.

The rep and her manager were apparently speaking to Raiko when two men came in and asked whether he was the owner of a green Renault car parked round the corner. When Raiko confirmed that the car belonged to him, the men said they were terribly sorry but they'd accidentally bumped into the car while parking. If he'd like to step outside now, they could assess the likely damage immediately. Having no reason to suspect that the gentlemen were lying, naturally Raiko did as they suggested – only to find himself handcuffed, under arrest and on his way to Bury Police Station the moment he stepped outside the door.

Now the two representatives were left alone in the shop with just Tracy, our Jewish assistant, for company. A few moments later, however, Tracy was approached by two young ladies who asked to see the white basque displayed in the window.

'Come outside and we'll show you which one it is,' they said. Once she was outside, they had arrested her too. Just imagine the scene! These two poor reps had just seen Raiko disappear without explanation, then Tracy. Now they watched spellbound as three burly men burst into the shop, bounded up the stairs and then came marching down with a bemused me and a shame-faced, cringing man in tow.

Several minutes passed. No one appeared. The ringing phones went unanswered. They stood there, alone, unsure of what to do and gradually convincing themselves that they were the unwitting victims of a candid camera stunt. For half an hour they tentatively answered what were undoubtedly some of the strangest telephone calls they had ever received, and then, unable to fathom out what was going on, they departed too, leaving an empty, unlocked shop with nobody to guard either the premises or the full till other than my beloved Sheba.

When I arrived at Bury Police Station I was put into an interview room and subjected to the indignities of having all the personal belongings in my handbag checked through, my jewellery removed and my body searched before being put into a filthy, rank cell which contained only a hard, concrete bunk with an inch-thin plastic-covered mattress and a stinking old army blanket. Mercifully there was at least a toilet, though it lacked all accompanying refinements such as a seat, toilet paper and any handle by which it could be flushed. However, when I discovered that there was a spyhole strategically placed in the door through which I could be observed, I rather lost the urge for relief!

It was four hours before anyone came along to take a statement, and during that time I'd been given nothing to eat or drink. Eventually I was taken outside to make a statement. I asked if I could at least call a member of staff to lock up the shop and ensure that Sheba was fed for the night, and grudgingly this was agreed.

The police officers who took down my statement were amazed at my frankness. Without prompting I told them everything I had been doing for the past year and why, because I didn't see any reason why I shouldn't be honest with them. The only information I flatly refused to supply was the names of my clients.

'We have a tape recording of you offering sexual services to a police officer,' one of them accused.

'I didn't just offer them to police officers,' I said, seeing no reason to lie. 'I offered them to everybody.'

I was then taken to another room, photographed with a

number across my chest, fingerprinted for posterity and then returned to my cheerless cell where I was served with a soggy offering of corned beef accompanied by a few (very few) french fries. The conditions, the filth and the extreme cold and loneliness were indescribable. Several times I asked for another blanket before I was eventually given one every bit as filthy as the first. Later on there was a scuffling noise and a great deal of bad language as another victim was bundled into a cell.

Banging loudly on the wall, I said to the officer, 'I don't wish to be awkward, but I find your swearing highly offensive.' The poor man was so taken aback that he blushed and apologized.

As the night wore on, I began to despair. Where were Raiko and Tracy? Would Sheba be all right on her own? And then, Oh my God! What on earth would David say when he found out!

It was time to take one of my daily hormone pills, but even this simple request was denied. Now I was becoming angry.

'Right, then,' I said to the sergeant. 'Are you prepared to sign a declaration stating that you accept full responsibility for withholding prescribed medical treatment from me?'

Confronted with such determination, the sergeant retreated for a hasty conference with his superiors, who decided that he had better let me take my pill. Considering that Britain is a country where the law presumes a person's innocence until he or she is found guilty, such behaviour was shocking. Finally a call was put through on my behalf to my solicitor, who made sufficient fuss to ensure that I at least received the items of make-up that Karen had brought in so that I could make myself presentable before the following morning's appearance in court.

I spent a fitful night, dozing and worrying about Raiko, Tracy, Sheba, David and the shop, huddled in my thin summer dress beneath the two disgusting blankets. In the morning, I was shepherded out to a waiting van where I found Raiko, wearing handcuffs and minus his shoes. I was outraged – I just couldn't believe that they would have the nerve to force such an inoffensive person as Raiko to wear handcuffs and that they had even had the gall to remove his shoes in case he should try to hang himself with his shoelaces. The whole affair was beginning to seem quite ludicrous and very obviously mismanaged.

Four hours later we were formally charged with keeping a bawdy house. It was an ancient piece of legislation, so rarely invoked that my solicitor could hardly be blamed for having advised me in the first place that I wasn't breaking the law. Geoff, who had given me the misguided advice that I wasn't breaking the law, represented us in court and immediately managed to get us out on unconditional bail with a hearing set for the following month. It was with great relief that we stumbled out into the sunshine and were taken to our respective homes in Geoff's car.

The first thing I needed was a bath. I felt so filthy that I didn't think I would ever feel clean again. I hugged Sheba, who accompanied me upstairs and stayed with me as if to protect me while I stripped off and scrubbed myself clean.

Now I had to face the worst ordeal of all: I had to telephone David and confess what had happened – and I had to do it fast because the local radio station were broadcasting half-hourly bulletins recounting the story of my arrest. Trembling, I picked up the telephone and dialled David's number. I was so nervous that I have absolutely no recollection of what I said or even how I said it. All I know is that I stumbled over my words, sobbing and begging David to believe that I had only done it in order to save the business.

David listened patiently while I rambled on, and when I eventually ran out of words he cleared his throat and said in measured tones: 'Stephanie, I believe you did the wrong thing ... but for the right reason.' If he had shouted at me, told me off, called me a silly bitch or any other kind of name I could have taken it, but to hear those kind, understanding words reduced me to tears all over again.

'Stephanie, I'll call round later and we'll discuss it then,' David said.

Of course the media had a field day – every paper carried the story of my disgrace and it even made the evening TV news. When David called round that evening I cried copiously on his shoulder, convinced I had made a mess of everything. I felt sure that we would now be boycotted by all our legitimate customers, hounded by the media, reviled by the neighbours and forced to allow our little business to shrivel up and die. I was absolutely mortified to see the results of my actions, and I blamed myself totally for dragging my two best and dearest friends down with me into the mire. But David and Raiko were wonderful, refusing to allow me to take the blame or to martyr myself. But though I was grateful for their unswerving devotion and their loyalty and support, I could only dread what the future now held in store. Once again, I was in a situation where things looked as if they had never been bleaker.

10
LAST LOVE

The effect on our business and our lives was immediate. Suppliers suddenly started experiencing 'problems' with the fulfilment of our orders, goods failed to turn up, and many of the people with whom we had previously traded quite happily and satisfactorily began to find excuses for not being able to trade with us at all now. All our female customers deserted us, apart from one or two stragglers who were motivated more by curiosity than by any desire to remain loyal.

Clearly, we could no longer continue trying to cater for both the male and female market; there were enough other beauty parlours around to take care of the women who no longer wanted to be associated with us, but very few, if any, outlets catering exclusively to the male transvestite market. Theoretically, the decision was an easy one to make; practically, however, the problems that the publicity was causing us had the potential to scupper all our well-laid plans. But they say there's no such thing as bad publicity, and though our arrest seemed like a disaster at the time it soon transpired that the publicity had achieved the one thing we had never been able to do – it had promoted the nature of our business to a nationwide audience, and within days we were deluged with mail from transvestites requesting information on the products we supplied.

Naturally, the neighbours were appalled to think that they had had a practising prostitute living in their midst all this time. Tongues wagged, curtains twitched and the 'strange goings-on' down Bury Old Road became the hottest topic of the year. We had a visit from a local council official who informed us that we were trading illegally by opening on Sundays and that in future we could only stay open until eight in the evening on weekdays with just one late-night opening till nine. Several attempts were made to get our shop classified as a 'sex shop', to which I responded by stating that I had no objections to this classification providing Marks and Spencer, Dorothy Perkins and all the other shops and stores retailing female lingerie were reclassified too!

Obviously, my extra-curricular activities ceased the moment

I was arrested. Frankly I wasn't too unhappy, because I was quite looking forward to the fresh challenge that lay in front of me: putting into operation some of the many plans that Raiko, David and I had for expanding our business, moving into publishing and setting up a mail order operation.

David's wife, Ethel was absolutely furious when she read the newspapers, and commanded him to withdraw his financial backing and sever his connections with Raiko and myself. But David, being David, calmly told Ethel that he saw no good reason for dissolving such a good business partnership. Then Ethel played her trump card. She gave him an ultimatum: 'Either break off this business relationship or we're finished.'

None of this was made known to me until several weeks had passed, which again is a measure of the kind of man David is, for he'd no more consider dumping his problems on other people than he would going back on his word. Now that there were no barriers between us, David, Raiko and I began to spend more time together planning the new direction our business was to take; and, whilst David still continued to run his supermarkets and have little day-to-day involvement in Transformation, the three of us inevitably grew closer as friends.

One Tuesday evening, when David called round for his normal weekly update on the business, he finally informed me in a typically understated fashion that he was experiencing domestic problems.

'What kind of domestic problems, David?' I enquired, thinking he would tell me of some little difficulty he and Ethel might be having with one of their daughters.

'Ethel's given me an ultimatum: Transformation or divorce.'

My stomach turned over as the full implication of David's simple statement sank in. 'Then you *must* pull out of Transformation, David. Raiko and I will do all we can to repay your investment, although it might take us years before we're in a position to repay you in full.'

Characteristically, David made no further comment and merely carried on discussing how far we had got with our new business plan. When David left I immediately rang Raiko to inform him of this latest turn of events. Although the prospect of losing David as a business partner was a bitter blow professionally, both of us felt equally devastated at the thought of losing him as a friend. Moreover, I just couldn't understand Ethel's extreme reaction: 'How can anyone put the person they love in such a position, Raiko?' I asked in despair.

With wisdom far beyond his years, Raiko merely replied: 'Because Ethel obviously *doesn't* love David, Stephanie.'

Knowing there was nothing we could do that wouldn't make matters worse for David, Raiko and I agreed that, as neither of us wanted to make his life more difficult or complicated than we had seemingly already done, we should leave it up to David to dictate what should be done and how.

David continued to make his Tuesday night visits to the flat, but made no more mention of Ethel's ultimatum. Naturally I was concerned for David's sake, but I didn't feel that it was up to me to raise the subject with him. Then one evening, six weeks later, he arrived looking tired, scruffy and slightly the worse for wear.

'David, what's wrong with you? You look as if you've been sleeping rough,' I chided him.

Without a word David produced from his briefcase a solicitor's letter asking him to vacate the marital home. Then the whole story came tumbling out. I listened in horror as David told me how he had been sleeping on the floor of his office for the past four nights and living on biscuits and snacks.

'For Christ's sake, David, why didn't you tell us? You're a shareholder in this business. You have every right to seek our support and help. You know there's a spare bedroom here that you could have used.'

I was very upset that David hadn't confided in either Raiko or myself, and ashamed and mortified that we hadn't had the insight to see how bad things really were for him. Throughout the time I had known him, and no matter what I had been through or done, David had never offered me anything other than kindness, generosity and support. I wanted to do whatever I could for him now, in his hour of need.

Briskly, I started ordering him around. 'Right, get out of those clothes and into the bath. I'm going to wash your shirt and underwear, press your suit and cook you a good square meal.' Too tired to argue or resist, David meekly did as he was told.

Refreshed by his bath and relieved at finally having shared his problems with someone, David allowed his tongue to loosen as we shared a bottle of good red wine over dinner. Soon he was pouring out all the details of the unhappy years of his marriage – Ethel's apparent disinterest in sex, her lapses on two occasions when she had left him for another man and, finally, that the only reason he had stayed with Ethel was for the sake of their children.

Ashamed, I could only reflect on how vastly I had under-estimated this man. I had – wrongly, I now knew – assumed that he would dissolve our partnership, but clearly his commitment to Transformation, Raiko and myself was far more binding than I had ever imagined. Like a mother hen, I made up a bed in the spare room and shooed David off for a good night's rest. As I lay in my own bed, unable to sleep, all I could think about was how unfair life was and how it always seemed that the nicest of people were appreciated the least. Maternal feelings welled up in me: I wanted to look after David, to protect him from the world, to offer comfort and to hold him – and to tell him that I, at least, cared. Impulsively I rose from my bed, slipped into my dressing gown and knocked on David's bedroom door.

'Can't you sleep, either?' I said when he invited me in.

'No.'

'Then why don't you come into my bed and stay awake with me?'

Taking him by the hand, I drew David out of his room and into my own. We lay together in the darkness, our arms loosely draped around one another as we talked and I tried to offer what comfort I could. Then our embrace tightened and we were kissing. Within moments we were making passionate love. After-wards, we talked some more and then, slowly, gently and in total contrast to his previous wild abandon, David made love to me a second time.

From that moment on there was no question of David ever going home again. We continued to live together and from a firm basis of friendship and trust, our love for one another slowly grew and grew into total devotion and commitment.

The following Sunday I invited Raiko to join me on my daily walk with Sheba in the park. We stopped to buy an ice cream, and as we sat there enjoying the glorious sunshine I told him what had happened between David and myself, desperately wanting – and needing – his approval. In the event Raiko was delighted for us, though he couldn't resist impishly declaring: 'At least now we can keep *all* the shares in the family!'

While we were waiting for a trial date to be scheduled, David and I decided that it made sense to sell off his smaller super-markets and open larger ones that would trade all day and all evening every day throughout the year. Terrified that the police might try and harass me if I appeared still to be involved in Transformation, I officially resigned as a director and kept a low profile, basing myself at our Stockport supermarket. In fact I was still very much involved in the marketing side of the business, only now I was running things behind the scene. Working in the supermarket with David provided the perfect opportunity for me to stay out of reach of the police. As in everything we have done together since, David and I both put in the same amount of effort and hard work. Before long the lovely, lazy Sunday I had so briefly enjoyed became a thing of the past as I worked with David in the supermarket from eight in the morning till ten at night, seven days a week.

On Monday, 2 December 1985 Raiko and I were finally hauled up in court. However, despite the fact that they'd had nine months to prepare, the police still hadn't managed to file all the necessary papers on time. The judge was obviously so annoyed and exasperated by the police and the prosecution's bungling of the whole affair that, much to my amusement and their dismay, he actually gave them a public ticking off in court before adjourning the trial for 24 hours to give himself time to read all the information that had been compiled against me.

Back we went the next day. This time, we were approached by the police before the trial even started. They wanted to do a deal: in return for changing my plea from not guilty to guilty they'd drop all charges against Raiko. But Raiko was insistent that I should not be allowed to take all the blame. I argued the point on the grounds that Raiko had a family whose lives would be affected if he was found guilty, while the only person who would be affected if I were convicted would be David – and we knew he'd stand by me no matter what ensued. Besides, I pointed out, if Raiko were free at least he could take care of the business if I did get a prison sentence. Privately, we both felt that we stood a very good chance of getting acquitted, but in the end the safest bet seemed to be to accept the deal.

My barrister submitted a plea of mitigation, during which he recounted in melodramatic detail all the misfortunes of my unusual life and stressed the fact that we *had* taken the best legal advice available and had sincerely believed that what we proposed to do was not illegal. Furthermore, he pleaded, the fact that we had been so open about our activities was surely proof enough that we were genuinely convinced we had been complying with the law.

Then came the moment I'm sure every defendant dreads; the actual summing up and sentencing by the judge. I knew the law did not recognize me as a woman, so if I was found guilty I would be sent to a male prison. The thought of the horrors that would undoubtedly befall me there made me feel faint. It also struck me as ludicrous that I could be charged as a female prostitute plying her trade and then be sentenced as a man!

After stating that, whilst all the evidence had proved that my transgressions had been committed in complete ignorance of the law, ignorance was no plea in relation to the law and therefore was not recognized by the law, the judge looked me straight in the eye and solemnly declared: 'Stephanie Anne Lloyd, I sentence you to twelve months' imprisonment suspended for twelve months.' He then went on to say that he was not imposing any fines and that all costs were awarded against the Crown. By this time, however, I was in such a state of shock that I was totally unable to comprehend what was happening. Seeking some interpretation of what had just occurred, I looked across at Raiko's jubilant face in the public gallery. But it was only when the prison officer standing behind me moved forward to touch me on the shoulder and inform me that I was free to go that I realized I wasn't actually heading for a cell.

As Raiko and I hugged each other, with a mixture of elation and disbelief, the media swooped. That evening all the local papers had a field day. The *Bolton Evening News* devoted its entire front page and part of page two to reporting every sordid little detail, and the following day the *Sun* broadcast the story under the headline: 'CALL ME MADAM – Sex-swap executive became a vice queen'. No matter how much I hated it, it seemed I was forever destined to be front page news.

As always, David proved to be a tower of strength and a tremendous comfort to me, telling me that in a few days the story would be yesterday's news and life would soon return to normal for us. But as it turned out, our problems were still far from being over. The very next day David received a telephone call from his father, who bluntly asked him whether he was the mysterious 'other businessman' mentioned in the articles about me. As always, David was unable to lie. When he told me what had transpired I saw immediately how upset he was, and it didn't take much imagination to understand how distraught his parents must be too.

'There's only one thing to do, David,' I said. 'We should go over there straightaway, and I must tell your father the whole story myself.'

David's father, who lived with his second wife in Bolton, had been far from pleased when David and Ethel had split up. So I could imagine only too well how he must be feeling now that he had discovered that not only was David living with another woman who had undergone a sex change operation, but that that same woman was also a convicted prostitute...! In the light of that knowledge, the fact that David's parents agreed to see me at all was nothing short of a miracle.

'All I ask of you,' I said, 'is that you give me an hour to tell you my story.' I then gave David's parents a brief résumé of my life story over a pot of tea. When I had finished, I merely said: 'And I'd like to reassure you that, no matter what you might think afterwards, I don't want *anything* ever to come between you and your relationship with David.'

To their credit and my astonishment, David's parents sat in silence while I told them all the details. Even more remarkably, they didn't reject me out of hand when I had finished. Whatever their private fears for their son and their thoughts about me, they made a decision to give me a chance to prove my love for David and, in doing so, to prove myself to them.

Now, they see us still happy with one another, still very much in love and still totally committed to a future together – and these two exceptional people have, I know, taken me as much to their hearts as I have taken them to mine. How many people, I sometimes ask myself, would have been so tolerant and accepted me so openly and warm-heartedly as these dear parents-in-law of mine? And how very lucky I am to have found not only a husband as wonderful as David, but two loving new parents as well! When I consider my good fortune, it makes me feel humble and I can only marvel at the proof they have all given to me: that given time and the opportunity, love can indeed transcend all problems and barriers.

With the traumas of the trial and David's difficulties with his parents now behind us, our life together began to take on a new sweetness. One evening when we were in bed together after a celebratory meal with Raiko, David took me in his arms and whispered words that took my breath away: 'Stephanie, I love you. Will you marry me?' I could hardly believe my ears. David had never before said the words 'I love you', though his actions had never left me in any doubt that he did. My response was to burst into tears. Poor David didn't know what to think as my sobs made incoherent nonsense of my attempts to say 'yes'.

Much later, as David lay sleeping, I gazed at his dear face and marvelled at my incredible good fortune in having met this man who had come to mean so very much to me. Contrary to what people who don't know David often imagine, he was – and is – a normal, well-adjusted, heterosexual male. He's also considerate, thoughtful and probably the most dependable person I've ever met in my entire life. I knew beyond a shadow of a doubt that David wasn't interested in me out of some bizarre form of curiosity. He didn't want me for money, for power or for anything else other than pure love, and that he should not only love me – a person whom most of the world had rejected – but had every intention of proving his love in the eyes of a disbelieving world by actually marrying me struck me as quite the most astonishing miracle that had ever happened to me. As I lay there that night, mentally hugging myself with unbelievable joy, I resolved that whatever else I did in my life, my first priority would be always to make David happy.

Accepting David's proposal was the easiest thing in the world for me, but actually marrying him in the eyes of both the church and the law of England was, of course, quite impossible. My birth certificate (which can never be changed under current British law) proclaimed I was a man, and therefore legally I could only ever marry a female.

David went to great lengths to seek expert legal advice and was advised that, though there were some countries in which we could be legally married, our marriage would never be officially recognized in Britain. Confirmation of that fact, however, merely served to increase David's efforts to find a way for us to get married. In February 1986 we flew to Sri Lanka armed with all the necessary documentation, and on 14 February, Valentine's Day, we finally became husband and wife in what, for me, will always remain one of the most romantic locations in the world.

I had brought a beautiful off-white dress with me to wear for the ceremony and, despite our one regret that our families and closest friends could not be with us, we had a perfect wedding. Strangers quickly became friends, so there were no difficulties in finding witnesses to fulfil the legal requirements. As we stood there together, the thought ran through my mind, 'Could this man who had already brought so much happiness and joy into my life *really* want me as his wife? Could he be so *sure* of his love for me that he would bind himself to me for the rest of our lives?' All my doubts were swept away when David said the immortal words, 'I do.' I tearfully echoed David's pronouncement and happily committed the remainder of my life to the man who had taught me what true love really means.

Our fairytale honeymoon was to be the last break David and I were to have together in a long, long time, for once we returned to England we both knew that all our energies would have to be concentrated on turning Transformation from a fledgeling company that showed promise into the kind of multi-faceted empire we both knew it had the potential to become.

Gradually our self-imposed punishing schedule of working long hours seven days a week began to pay off, but on the personal front we were still beset by problems. David's ex-wife, Ethel, refused to be content with the generous settlement she had received on their divorce, and when their teenage daughter, Lisa, left home to move in with us after yet another argument with her mother, Ethel's bitterness and dissatisfaction got out of hand.

As a loving and devoted father, David had fought for access to Lisa and her sister, Dawn. Despite Ethel's attempts to wage a bitter war against us, primarily on the grounds that I was a bad influence, both girls had maintained that they wished to see both their father and myself. Their statement had gone a long way towards convincing the courts that as I was not a threat David should be allowed to see his daughters and bring them to our home, the only proviso being that we would not be allowed to take Lisa and Dawn out of the country together. Effectively, this meant that if David wanted to take the girls on holiday abroad I would not be allowed to accompany them. Though neither of us could work out the reasoning behind such a judgement, it seemed like a small price to pay at the time.

I still missed my own children dreadfully and, though Lisa and Dawn could never replace Stephen, Andrew and Becky in my heart, we soon developed a warm, friendly relationship which helped to assuage the pain and sorrow I still felt at missing so much of my own children's growing years. From the very first, though, I laid down some ground rules with the girls.

'Two parents are enough to wish on any child,' I told them frankly. 'Therefore I have no wish to replace your mother, or even to be a stepmother to you both. You have one mother – you don't need another. But I would like to be your friend.' And that's exactly what we have become: friends.

Soon afterwards Lisa had an almighty row with her mother, after which we received a telephone call from Ethel announcing that she was bringing Lisa over 'with all her things'. So at two in the morning Lisa was dumped on our doorstep with five carrier bags, and she stayed with us for several months.

Unfortunately, the knowledge that Lisa was quite content to stay with us for several months must have been the last straw for poor Ethel. A few months later we received a telephone call from a reporter working on the *Sunday People* who claimed to have been given a story by the ex-Mrs Booth, alleging that David had not only left her penniless and stolen her daughter, but that she was living in penury in a council flat (after having been evicted 'because David had not kept up the mortgage payments' on their house) while we were living like millionaires! I was outraged. The truth was that David had signed the house over to Ethel and had made a substantial financial settlement which she had been advised to accept by no less than five different solicitors whom she had consulted in turn. All of this I coolly pointed out to the reporter.

'If you don't believe me,' I said, 'I will give you the names of both her solicitor and ours, and you can check the facts out for yourself.'

Two weeks later a damaging – and patently untrue – story appeared in the *Sunday People*, outlining Ethel's account. I was incensed, because not only was there not one grain of truth in the report, but they clearly hadn't bothered to check any of the facts or to print one word of David's version. I wasn't bothered for my own sake, but I was very angry on David's behalf. Immediately I complained to the Press Council, and after much fighting, wrangling and a large number of solicitor's letters flying back and forth a hearing was set. And what a farce it was! Suffice it to say that, while the *Sunday People* were rebuked for not bothering to check the facts, the complaint was not upheld. I'm afraid that none of my brushes with British law or the Establishment have caused me to revise my opinion that British law is laughable and that there is no such thing as honour, truth and justice when it comes to the British press.

Following the acrimony over Ethel's lies David decided we all needed a break, but as I was banned from leaving the country with him and Lisa we were forced to take separate holidays. He and Lisa would go to Greece together while I would travel to Portugal on my own.

Although I missed David terribly, I resolved to make the best of things and enjoy the rest and sunshine. One day I booked to go on a boat trip in the company of various other holidaymakers who were staying at different resorts. During the coach journey I became friendly with a couple who were on holiday with their five young children, one of whom took a shine to me. I had an enjoyable day swimming in the sea with this little lad and playing with his brothers and sisters on the beach. The parents, who said they ran a restaurant in Wigan, seemed like a nice couple and we all got on very well together. However, when it was time to rejoin the coach we were late arriving at the meeting point as several of the children had wanted to go to the lavatory at the last moment. When we did finally arrive, we found that the coach had left without us. So we hired a taxi to take us back to the hotel where my new friends were staying, and then went for a late meal in a nearby café.

'Don't worry,' the husband said to me. 'I've got a hire car and I'll run you back to your hotel.' During the meal the drinks flowed more liberally than perhaps they should have, so by the time I climbed into the passenger seat of the man's car I was beginning to have a few doubts about his ability to drive.

In retrospect, I should have refused his offer and taken a taxi, but as we'd all had such a pleasant day together and I didn't really want to offend him I accepted the lift. If ever there was a decision I regretted in my life, that was it – for halfway through the journey, and without any prior warning, he pulled the car over to the side of the road and launched himself upon me. Nothing in the entire history of my strange life could have prepared me for the horror of what then ensued. In a word, it was rape. And though I'm big and strong for a woman, I'm still no match for a man as the female hormones I take have caused a certain amount of muscle wastage and weakened me. I was in such a state of shock at the suddenness of my assailant's attack that, despite my protests and my efforts to fight him off, he accomplished his objective.

Immediately it was over, he drove me back to my hotel and unceremoniously dumped me in the street. I was so upset and so bewildered that I couldn't say a word – I just rushed straight upstairs to my room and threw myself on to my bed. Words can't describe what I felt. I was far too shocked and dazed to feel dirty or even humiliated at that stage, because my numbed brain couldn't believe that such a thing had happened to me.

Eventually I was able to summon up enough sense to complain to the courier who, though exceedingly sympathetic, was none the less all too well aware of the futility of trying to invoke the Portugese legal system.

'Of course you can prosecute,' she said. 'But I have to warn you that it will involve a trial here, and as it could take months before it goes to court you may well find yourself not being able to leave the country in the meantime.'

'I just want to go home,' I wailed in despair.

'Then perhaps the best thing you could do would be to forget about it . . . if you can.'

I was due to return home in three days. All I wanted was to be safe and secure once more in David's arms. The thought of having to stay in Portugal for months, and of all the unwelcome publicity that such a court case would undoubtedly attract, was beginning to frighten me far more than the actual rape itself. Then another thought occurred to me: as legally I was still a man, what were the chances of a successful conviction? After all, it was well known that in the eyes of the law men can't possibly be raped!

My principles warred with my desire to crawl away and forget the horrific incident. And in the end that's precisely what I did, though I'm not sure it's something I will ever be able truly to forget – as any woman who has been the victim of such a grossly personal invasion will confirm.

I got through the next few days like a zombie and throughout the journey home I was withdrawn and tearful. Obviously I was still in a state of extreme shock. The moment I saw Raiko I just fell into his arms and sobbed out all the sordid details. He was as outraged and as shocked as I had been. I didn't know whether to tell David or not – one half of me needed the kind of consolation that only his patient love and support could provide, whilst the other part of me felt dirty, humiliated and deeply ashamed.

In the event David's plane was delayed, and by the time he did eventually get home I was in such a state that it was obvious to him that something was terribly wrong. David was, as usual, wonderful, and his love and concern did much to erase the horror from my mind, but we did vow that we would never take separate holidays again.

11
THE PHOENIX RISES

Having long before reached the conclusion that there was a vast untapped market to explore in the secret, hidden world of transvestism, David, Raiko and I agreed that while David would continue to concentrate all his efforts on the supermarkets, Raiko and I would spend the next few months researching and planning the next vital steps in the growth of the Transformation side of the business. When our plans for a mail order catalogue were finalized, Raiko and I turned our hands to sketching out a rough visual layout and writing the necessary copy. Now, all we had to do was hire the models and find a photographic studio willing to take on such an unusual project.

After several rejections we eventually found Studio Alexander whose proprietors, Leslie and Clifford, were prepared to undertake the photography for our catalogue on a fixed-budget basis. Our financial resources were so tight that every single penny had to be well spent. On the first day of the shoot we arrived at the studio accompanied by six of the best page three girls in the business, and though it was a long and arduous two weeks, we were all delighted and exhilarated when we saw the results of our work on celluloid.

Some of the models we hired for that first catalogue have since gone on to become very famous. Lou Varley was just sixteen at the time, so her parents' permission had to be sought for her to pose topless, but she has since carved out a very successful and lucrative career for herself. Gail McKenna was another model on that first shoot who soon became one of the UK's top glamour models. I have to say that, far from being bitchy and competitive, as I had been led to believe, all the girls who worked on our catalogue proved to be tremendous fun, very friendly and extremely professional indeed.

Our next venture was to launch a small adult contact magazine called *Connections*, which proved to be unique in that we not only accepted all advertisements free of charge but also forwarded all replies to the advertisers at our own expense. The fact that our magazine was so glossy and well produced in comparison to the competition also contributed greatly to its success.

Our second launch, another contact magazine, *Direct Connect* (so named because we featured actual telephone numbers), was a far more ambitious project. Every single 'contact' had to be checked and verified in order to weed out those who might be seeking financial rewards for services, any potential 'perverts', the 'time-wasters' – who delighted in giving false names and addresses – and, of course, to ensure that every advertisement complied with both the current legal requirements and our own ethical standards.

Our expansion into such diverse businesses as publishing, mail order, retailing and groceries provided an opportunity to utilize all the skills and expertise I had acquired over the years, and it wasn't long before the results of our intensive marketing efforts began to pay off. When commercial success finally came, it came on all fronts. Thus we were able to form the strong foundation on which our group of companies is now based.

The supermarkets were open all hours seven days a week and we used every possible concept to promote the fact – from loss leaders to silly ten pence offers at traditionally slack times. We even organized events such as pancake races around the store, and soon we were welcoming a steady stream of traffic through our doors from the moment we opened at eight in the morning right up until we closed at ten at night. Although our opening times meant a great deal of hard work for all three of us (including having to man the tills every Christmas Day in order to give the staff a day off), the formula proved to be an enormous success.

One problem we experienced, however, was with Stockport Council, who regularly sent officers into our stores on Sundays to purchase prohibited items such as dog food or frozen foods. Whilst many councils ignore Sunday trading, there are still some who insist on enforcing the law. Obviously this creates a situation in which legal anomalies abound; to my mind it's a bit like being allowed to speed on motorways in Yorkshire but to risk prosecution for doing so in the Home Counties. By its very nature, operating self-service food stores as large as ours makes it virtually impossible to police an archaic law which dictates that people can legally purchase cigarettes, alcohol and girlie magazines on a Sunday but are not able to buy cough medicine, frozen foods or anything that comes in cans. Try telling a customer that he can have his eggs for breakfast but you won't sell him the bacon to go with it, and see whether he ever shops with you again!

Inevitably we were hauled before the courts and charged with unlawfully selling a tin of dog food and a packet of washing powder, for which we were fined the outrageous sum of £600. The case which preceded ours involved a drunk driver who had crashed his car. His fine was just £150. So, by definition, it is four times more serious to sell a can of dog food on a Sunday than to risk killing someone whilst driving under the influence of alcohol! One more nail in the coffin for British justice.

Having identified a huge gap in the transvestite market, we now developed the ambitious concept of *TV Scene* – a lavishly produced, glossy, 52-page magazine which would feature colour photography as well as in-depth investigative articles on topics ranging from hormones and transvestism to the law and sex-change operations. At that point we decided to form a separate company to cope with our fast-expanding publishing division, which by now had taken over the entire flat with the exception of our bedroom. Just when we started looking for suitable alternative premises a suite of first-floor offices right across the road came on to the market. This was the humble start of our head office, which today stretches right across the top of that same building and seven others on either side.

Production of the first issue of *TV Scene* began in earnest, and as we knew the costs of launching would be astronomical it was decided that, in order both to keep the costs at a realistically affordable level and to come up with something sufficiently startling to promote it, nude photographs of me should form the basis of the lead story. After all, I was by now quite famous – or infamous, if you like – and there was bound to be a great deal of prurient interest in what 'Sex Change Stephanie Anne Lloyd' looked like in the flesh.

Studio Alexander again undertook the assignment, with Leslie himself shooting the photographs behind locked studio doors and with the bare minimum of people present – one of whom was (at her own request) Lisa, my eldest stepdaughter. Thus, at the ripe old age of forty-one, I added yet another experience to my life. The final photographs were truly stunning, and shot so tastefully that I could find no reason to be ashamed of the fact that they not only adorned the pages of the launch issue of *TV Scene*, but were subsequently acquired by a national Sunday newspaper and published on its centrefold! Once again I received a great deal of criticism (mainly from women who accused me of grossly exploiting my new-found femininity), but on that occasion it didn't bother me in the least as *I* knew I was the only nude model we could afford.

Shortly afterwards I was asked to appear on a television programme to debate the issue of man's exploitation of glamour models. Also present was an extremely beautiful young lady called Miranda, who had recently received £15,000 for three days' work posing for nude photographs destined for publication in *Penthouse*. When asked whether I agreed with the notion that Miranda was being exploited by men, I'm afraid I could only smile wryly and say: 'It's extremely difficult to feel Miranda has been exploited by men when they're the very ones who have just parted with a rather large sum of money in return for such an exceptionally short period of work!'

From such small beginnings our mighty oak tree grew . . . and continued to grow. Now we are not only one of the most successful – and prolific – publishers in the UK, but also the largest supplier of specialist adult contact magazines, books and videos of specific interest to the transvestite and female-domination markets, with over 150 titles currently in print.

Meanwhile, the Transformation side of our business continued to increase as we slowly built up a relationship of trust and complete confidence with new customers, many of whom have since become part of our regular clientele. Despite much initial opposition from the press, who stubbornly refused to accept our advertising, a combination of legal threats, persuasion, persistence and a willingness to rewrite our copy whenever required has gradually helped us overcome their early resistance.

The fact that Raiko, David and myself all firmly believed in conducting as much research as possible before committing ourselves to a project has, in my opinion, contributed greatly to the success of our many business interests. For example, once we had discovered that our competitors' merchandise consisted solely of women's clothing, which was far from suitable for men who usually have much larger dimensions, we committed ourselves to the obvious step of manufacturing an exclusive range of correctly sized and shaped clothing specifically designed to feminize the male shape. Luck, too, played a part, in that the very moment we made this decision I happened to learn that the owner of the mill which manufactured some of our fashionwear was keen to divest himself of the worry of owning his own business but didn't want to retire altogether. We immediately struck a deal which would allow me to acquire the company without any initial payment on the proviso that, in return for guaranteeing him a job for life running the manufacturing operation, I would pay whatever I could afford as soon as I was in a position to afford it, with the eventual aim of buying him out altogether. It worked exceedingly well for both parties, and in fact this gentleman still continues to work for me despite the fact that he's now long past retirement age.

Working as hard as we were, time appeared to pass by very quickly indeed. Almost overnight, it seemed – though in reality it was much longer – the entire group was prospering to such an extent that we were able to invest some of our profits in the realization of several of my long-term ambitions.

First we opened a guest house in Prestwich, at which transvestites were able to take anything from a one-night break to a full week's holiday and be free to indulge in total privacy their love of living as women. We provided everything from clothes, wigs and shoes to instruction in make-up techniques, voice coaching and the subtleties of female deportment.

Immediately it became a huge success. I, for one, was not surprised. When you consider that there is so much prejudice and misunderstanding surrounding transvestism (which in 99 per cent of cases is nothing more than a relatively harmless interest), it was patently obvious that anyone who provided transvestites with a guaranteed safe haven in which they could relax and indulge the gentler aspects of their personalities would find themselves inundated with bookings. Word spread far wider than even we had anticipated, and it wasn't long before an Australian television company approached us with a request to make a documentary about a typical weekend at our hotel.

Joining our guests for dinner every evening after work became a regular part of David's and my routine, and invariably our guests would offer us their warmest thanks and heartfelt appreciation for providing them with what many of them came to regard as the only safe retreat they had. Our guests included people from all strata of society; there were bricklayers and labourers, policemen and judges, accountants and lawyers and even the head of one of Britain's largest nationalized industries.

Some of our guests were married, a few had even come with the blessing of their understanding and enlightened wives (in fact, for one delighted guest, a week's holiday with us had been the lovingly chosen surprise birthday present from his wife), but, sadly, the majority were men who were either forced to keep their 'secret' hidden from their wives or who had long since abandoned all hope of marriage for fear their prospective partners would never understand. It saddened me greatly that these men (who were otherwise totally normal, healthy, heterosexual males) were destined to live their lives hiding in a closet of fear and would probably never know the joys of a true partnership with the opposite sex. Surely, I thought, there must be *some* women, somewhere, who would be prepared to overlook this one 'interest' if they could be assured that in every other respect these men would make kind, loving, supportive husbands. As I mulled this over, an idea began to form. It led to the foundation of Orchid, a unique introduction agency for transvestites seeking sympathetic, understanding partners who would be more than happy to accept these men's interests as no more of a threat to a happy marriage than any other 'normal' hobby such as sport, photography or DIY.

As the word spread I was asked to do an interview with *Woman* magazine and, just as I had suspected, once the article appeared we were inundated with letters from women who had previously been married to drunken or violent men. Many of those letters confirmed my own thoughts: that a relationship with a man whose only 'fault' was dressing up in female clothes seemed infinitely preferable to the misery they had experienced in their dealings with so-called 'macho' men. When David and I were invited to the first wedding that Orchid was responsible for, we were overjoyed and truly felt as though we had accomplished something worthwhile.

My second ambition was realized when, after many months of searching for the right premises and a multitude of setbacks, we opened a branch in London right next to Euston Station and Transformation took its first step toward becoming a chain. From Day One our formula of offering quality goods and value for money, combined with a pleasant, helpful and understanding all-female staff who adhered strictly to our golden rule of customer confidentiality, was enough to ensure that we rapidly achieved market dominance. Since then, the Transformation chain has extended to Birmingham and Newcastle-upon-Tyne; plans for Scotland, Europe and, ultimately, America are on the drawing board.

Our experiences with the guest house confirmed that all transvestites need a safe place where they can dress and behave as women without fear of discovery. It's such a harmless thing to want, and yet it's the one thing they find virtually impossible to do. In order to meet that need we introduced another unique service, which we call TV Changeaways; these consist of four-hour sessions during which we provide absolutely everything to transform men into glamorous women. All the clothes, wigs and shoes are supplied by us, and our own highly trained beauticians make up each man's face. When the transformation is complete, the customers are free to roam the shop, chatting to, and having a drink with, the staff, sit upstairs in our luxurious Changeaway lounges and read magazines, watch TV or a video, or do virtually anything they want to do that provides them with a few peaceful hours away from prying eyes.

As I've said before, there is very little that could shock or surprise me about human nature, but one thing that never fails to confound me is the fact that so many very prominent men, particularly those in the legal profession, do so little to protect their identities. For example, we often get barristers in our London shop who will walk in with briefcases clearly displaying their initials; and I've lost count of the number of pinstripe-suited businessmen who come to us with a briefcase concealing female underwear or a pair of high-heeled shoes!

It's the nature of our business that we attract the unlikeliest of people, and it seems to me that neither class nor profession provide any protection when it comes to men's strange fetishes. We once had a man from London visit our Manchester shop late one evening when both Raiko and I were there alone. He undressed in a cubicle, donned all his favourite items of women's clothing including stockings, suspenders and high heels, expertly applied his make-up and then, as calmly as you please, informed us he was off for a drive around the neighbourhood and would we please keep an eye on his clothes.

Ten minutes later he came rushing back into the shop in an absolute panic, tears streaking rivulets of mascara-black lines down his carefully pan-sticked cheeks, words pouring out of his mouth in an unintelligible jumble. I took one look at Raiko, whose stunned expression mirrored my own. The man was so distressed he was incoherent. Eventually we managed to calm him down enough for him to be able to tell us what had upset him so. Apparently he'd left the shop happy as a sandboy (though sand*girl* would be more appropriate, I guess), tripping along the street in his six-inch heels, only to find when he turned the corner that his car was nowhere in sight – obviously it had been stolen.

'What will I do?' he wailed.

'Well, all you have to do is change back into your own clothes and then report it to the police,' I said, still not quite having grasped the enormity of this man's predicament.

'But you don't understand,' he wept. 'I *am* the police.'

'You're *what?*' shrieked Raiko and I in disbelieving unison.

'I'm a detective inspector with Scotland Yard,' the man explained, tearfully. 'And what's even worse: the boot of my car is full of your magazines and catalogues! If my colleagues find those, I'm ruined!'

We were both far too astonished to speak. Raiko went off to make the poor guy a cup of hot, strong, sweet tea while I tried to think up a plausible explanation for his predicament. We then persuaded him to clean off his make-up, change back into his ordinary clothes and then phone the local police station, saying he'd been in the neighbourhood, had stopped off for a pint, and when he'd returned to his car he'd discovered it had been stolen. As we had been the only shop still open at that time of night, he'd come in (not realizing, of course, what *kind* of shop we were) to ask whether we had seen or heard anything suspicious and to use our telephone.

Within half an hour a squad car arrived on our doorstep, and a posse of policemen took him off for a drive around the locality to see if they could find his missing car. We never did hear any more from him, though we've often wondered whether his vehicle was recovered and, if so, what happened about the cache of 'embarrassing naughties' concealed in the boot!

I've long since ceased to wonder, but I do occasionally ponder on the unusual enjoyments of some of our customers. I mean, what, for example, did the man we call 'The Jilted Bride' get out of his weekly outing around the park next door to one of our shops, dressed in full bridal rig complete with flowing headdress and white satin stilettos? Try as I might, I simply couldn't comprehend why dressing as a bride should give him such pleasure, but there he was, every Saturday without fail. My suspicions that he couldn't possibly find complete contentment in such curious and solitary behaviour were confirmed when, on one occasion, he offered Raiko a large sum of money if he would dress up in top hat and tails and accompany him on his weekly outing. Needless to say, Raiko, who finds such behaviour as mystifying as I do, couldn't bring himself to take part.

The interesting thing is, once a man has a particular fetish, no amount of money is spared in his attempts to find gratification. Take the Manchester-based man whom we christened the 'Satin Man', for example: he didn't look as if he had two ha'pennies to rub together judging by his appearance and the state of his everyday clothes, and yet every week he would turn up to purchase every single satin item we might have in stock, often buying the same items twice regardless of whether they were in his size or not. Furthermore, he always paid in good old-fashioned cash! He must have an entire wardrobe full of satin underwear by now – certainly far more than he could possibly ever have the opportunity to wear. But if a simple matter of quantity doesn't deter him, I don't suppose anything will.

Another customer who provided Raiko and me with many hours of speculation was the taxi driver who would come in every Wednesday morning to purchase a number of items, only to return again that afternoon and purchase exactly the same items all over again!

'What do you think he keeps buying the same items twice for?' I'd ask Raiko in puzzlement.

'Search me,' he'd reply. 'Perhaps he buys one lot for himself and then shows them to a friend who wants an identical set for himself.'

Eventually our curiosity got the better of us and we were compelled to find out more. The next time he came in I jokingly said, 'Here, you haven't got a twin brother by any chance, have you?' Just one look at his shocked expression was enough to tell us that we had accidentally hit the nail on the head.

'How d-did you know?' he stammered.

Raiko and I were so stunned that we could only exchange a weak smile and shrug. Imagine! Twin brothers, both with the same fetish and both apparently oblivious of their twin's secret! Though whether they're still oblivious after our blunder I wouldn't like to say – perhaps we even unwittingly did them both a favour. After all, they might be immensely relieved to know they're not alone!

Our group of businesses may have steadily grown on all fronts, but it hasn't all been plain sailing. In our case, many of the problems have been the direct result of the – to my mind, unreasoning – prejudice of many of our neighbours. Despite the fact that we conduct our business in an entirely professional manner, they none the less resented our presence in their midst and sought every opportunity to complain to the local council about the 'unrespectable goings-on' in Bury Old Road. In fact, I've lost count of the number of battles we have fought, the incidences of prejudice we've been subjected to and the sheer lack of tolerance that people still persist in displaying.

I've made it my practice to ignore prejudice and hostility as much as I can, but when it interferes with my life, my work or, indeed, any of the people I love or am responsible for, then I can become a formidable adversary. For when it comes to my principles I will choose to fight every time.

I'm well aware that many people will never be able to come to terms with the fact that there are other people in this world (and probably far more than any of us might imagine) who have sexual tastes or predilections outside the 'norm' (though I challenge anyone to tell me what 'normal' is). To those people, I and the business that I am involved in will always be considered 'beyond the pale', weird, abnormal, distasteful or, at the very least, unrespectable. Such people are, of course, perfectly entitled to their opinion – but, likewise, I am entitled to mine, which is that such opinions are based on ignorance and fear. Fear, because it is human nature to fear the unknown.

Though I'm no stranger to prejudice and intolerance, they still have the power to sadden me immensely. For prejudice and intolerance, which are born out of ignorance, breed hatred and resentment; and when these feelings are allowed to go unchecked, particularly on a global scale, war of one kind or another is often the result.

For my part, I don't have a problem regarding the nature of the business I run. We pay our taxes, we provide employment for a large number of people and we always inform the police if we come across anything unacceptable such as paedophilia. We have our own code of ethics; for example, we clearly state that no one under the age of eighteen is allowed to cross the threshold of any of our shops or to purchase any magazines or merchandise through our mail order operation. Furthermore, without exception every single person who works for us has to sign a contract which binds them to a strict code of confidentiality regarding our customers.

I do believe that I am contributing something worthwhile to society, and I have no doubt whatsoever that I am certainly responsible for bringing a little bit of happiness, comfort, understanding and perhaps even light into the lives of many people who, through no real fault of their own, might otherwise be feeling isolated and miserable. I understand that feeling because I have experienced it too. And having experienced it myself, I've always felt it would never be enough for me simply to empathize; somehow I had to find a way to do something concrete and positive to help anyone who feels as lonely, lost and confused as I once was myself.

Although our success has been built primarily on a foundation of hard work and a great deal of perspiration, I'm well aware that fortune has also played its part. After all, if I hadn't met Raiko or David none of the success we all presently enjoy would have been possible.

In 1987 I found myself reflecting on what a very long way I had come since the day Keith was transformed into Stephanie. As I recalled the personal and practical difficulties I had faced years earlier – the dearth of information, the relative lack of knowledge and sources of support available to people like myself – I knew the time had finally come for me to realize one of my dearest wishes.

That autumn the Albany Gender Identity Clinic was founded, specifically to offer counselling to people wishing to avail themselves of professional help in solving any problem they might have to do with their own gender. The clinic is a subsidized operation employing doctors and specialists trained in all the various aspects of gender identity problems, with counselling, support, medical advice and treatment available to all who need it. And although the clinic is based next to our offices in Manchester, it serves patients from all over the UK and abroad.

Although it is our ultimate aim to attain charitable status, for now the clinic's financial security is underwritten by the Maple Leaf Holdings Group, with much of the day-to-day running costs being defrayed by the medical slimming service for women that we run on certain days of the week. To see so many people who were confused, lost, lonely – and even on the point of suicide – smile again with hope as they leave our clinic is, for me, one of the most personally rewarding achievements of my life.

Inevitably I have attracted a great deal of media attention. Though much of it has been bad, it has also had the good effect of providing me with a platform from which I might have been able to strip away a little of the mystery, suspicion and prejudice that surround both transsexualism and transvestism. And if I have been able to remove even one person's fear, intolerance and prejudice, then I feel my notoriety has served a purpose.

I am not so naïve as to think that transvestism or transsexualism will ever become publicly acceptable, and I am resigned to the fact that for the rest of my life I will be considered a freak. But maybe one day mankind will learn to look deeper than the colour of a person's skin, or even beyond the nature of a person's sexual interests, and recognize the only thing that is of any importance: the kind of person one is inside.

It's interesting that the question I am most often asked is 'What type of person shows the most prejudice towards you?' My answer is: 'The person who does not know me.' Strangely enough, once people meet me and get to know me, they invariably recognize that I'm no different from anyone else: I'm not a two-headed ogre, I don't eat little children for breakfast, I'm not sick, depraved or perverted in any way – I'm simply a human being who, for whatever reason, was born to lead an unusual life. Apart from that I'm just like everyone else: I have feelings, emotions and a conscience, and I care deeply about the under-privileged, the handicapped, the misfits and the outcasts.

One thing I have learned is that, of all the negative characteristics man can have, prejudice is the single most destructive and demeaning trait of all. And that's why I have chosen to fight against prejudice (in whatever form it appears) as my own personal crusade, because no one should ever have to suffer victimization simply for being themselves – as I have. Over the past few years prejudice has threatened our business over and over again: our companies have been refused cover by one of the largest insurance companies in the UK; we were once stripped of our credit card facilities by a high street bank; we have even had a sizeable donation to one particular charity (to which every member of our staff had contributed with nine months' of fund-raising activities) spurned without explanation – and all because of who, and what, I am.

And yet, ironically, now that I am perceived to be successful, many of those same people who once vilified me as an 'unacceptable freak' now tolerate me as an 'acceptable eccentric'. Wealth, or lack of it, should never be of the least significance – but apparently it is. It's a sad, but telling, indictment of our society's values and of human nature.

I long ago came to terms with the fact that, no matter what I do, the 'doings' of 'Sex Change Stephanie' will always be newsworthy. And although I have never enjoyed the publicity I seem to generate, when I adopted the fight against prejudice as my own crusade against ignorance and fear, it occurred to me that my notoriety does, in fact, have a positive side.

On 9 December 1989 I did just that when I publicly fought – and won – a minor, but none the less significant, victory in a battle for equality between the sexes. For three years the issue of allowing women to become members of the Lancashire County Cricket Club had been raised at the LCC's Annual General Meeting, and each time it was defeated. Much controversy had raged in the press and, quite rightly, women's groups throughout the country were annoyed and frustrated at the blind arrogance of those men who still clung to the belief that women were not worthy of being admitted to their hallowed ranks.

About the same time I received a letter from the Inland Revenue (with whom I had been waging my own private war for recognition as a woman), which stated: 'Dear Miss Lloyd, whilst we have no doubts about your femininity, for tax purposes we must continue to treat you as a single male.' Knowing that I would never be able to change the fact that legally I was still regarded as a male was a constant source of frustration and irritation to me. However, as I sat at my desk, exasperated at this peremptory note, an idea began to take shape. If I was going to have to spend my entire life being officially classified as a male, might there not be some way of using that fact to solve another problem?

I duly applied to join the Lancashire County Cricket Club as Keith Michael Hull and, lo and behold, my application for membership was accepted. The next annual general meeting took place on 9 December and, armed with my birth certificate, a copy of the letter I had received from the Inland Revenue and (in accordance with club rules) dressed in a very smart velvet trouser suit, complete with silk shirt and tie, I attended the AGM – as was my right.

Fortunately, because of the amount of publicity the club had received in previous years, the TV crews were out in full force in anticipation of hordes of angry women demanding to be allowed membership. I waited until most of the members were seated in the meeting hall before entering the reception area. Immediately the TV crew jumped in front of me and a reporter said: 'Excuse me, madam, we're here to interview women about the fact that you are banned from membership of the club. Could we have your views?'

'But I'm a member,' I said. 'A fully paid-up member, and I *am* going in.' Not immediately realizing who I was, the TV crew obviously thought I must be some kind of nutcase and stopped filming while I marched up to the door, voting card in hand, and approached the steward.

'Sorry, madam, but you can't come in here,' he said, officiously.

'But I'm a member,' I smoothly replied.

The steward's face dropped. 'But...but you can't be...you're a *woman!*' he spluttered.

'Well, it seems the government disagrees with you. They don't regard me as a woman, and neither did your committee when they accepted my application for membership.'

I watched a multitude of expressions from discomfiture via panic to sheer horror cross the steward's face. I raised my eyebrows slightly and said: 'Now, here's my birth certificate, a letter from the government which clearly states that no matter what I might call myself, or how I might appear, I *am* legally still a male, my membership card and my voting card. Now, perhaps, you will kindly let me in.'

By this time the steward was beginning to look decidedly ill. Unsure about what action he could take next, he called the club secretary over and I had to go through the whole exercise again. Meanwhile, David, who (although he wasn't a member) had accompanied me as a gesture of support, slipped into the hall unnoticed. The club secretary sent for the president, who in turn sent for the club's solicitor, who took one look at me and declared: 'I don't know Miss Lloyd except by reputation, and all I can say is, if you don't admit her you are likely to have a writ on your desk first thing in the morning. And I'm telling you now, you will lose this case. You have no alternative but to let her in.'

Looking utterly defeated, the president's shoulders sagged, and with a great sigh he reluctantly uttered the immortal words: 'Let her in.'

Two thousand pairs of male eyes almost popped out of their sockets as, hair flowing down my back and looking every inch a woman, I walked down the central aisle and seated myself on a vacant chair. After several false starts the meeting began. Throughout the first hour I sat quietly listening with great interest to all the matters that were being discussed. Having accomplished my aim and forced the club to grant me admittance, I hadn't intended any other form of action. However, when the question of female membership was once again raised I took one look at the queue forming in front of the microphone in the centre of the aisle (I hadn't realized that members would be invited to address the meeting), and quite spontaneously stood up and took my place at the end of it.

The poor president took one look at me standing in the queue and visibly began to squirm. Then it was my turn to speak. 'Mr

President, ladies and gent...oh, I must apologize, I'm afraid I forgot that there *aren't* any ladies here.'

I referred to several of the objections that had been raised as valid reasons for keeping women out of the club and then tackled one that had really incensed me. 'One gentleman objected on the grounds that, if women were granted admittance, you'd soon have an army of kids running amok. What I would like to know is, who fathered these 'kids' whose presence you fear so much?' I paused, then simply stated: 'It would appear that the two thousand men present today all deny any involvement in the production of these children.'

You could have heard a pin drop.

'I'd also like to say that I find it rather, er, interesting, to note that though you regard yourselves as one of the last bastions of male dominance and supremacy, you none the less elected a mere female as your patron. Presumably, unlike me, your patron, The Queen, would *not* be granted admittance.'

The silence was deafening. Slowly, I looked around, gratified to note from the expressions on many faces that my comments had served to highlight the ridiculousness of the situation.

'Well, gentlemen, you *do* now have one *female* member of the LCC and, I'm afraid, there is nothing that you can do about it. So why not be sensible now, and cast your votes in favour of allowing the rest in.'

Having said all I had to say, there was nothing left for me to do but return to my seat. As I sat down, the elderly gentleman seated next to me leaned over, took my hand in his and with a gentle squeeze whispered to me: 'My dear, you are one very brave lady.'

When they had recovered from the shock, several men rushed forward to complain about my having been allowed publicly to address the meeting; but the president, knowing the true legal position, refused to acknowledge their protests. Then, to my surprise, one gentleman took the microphone and said: 'Mr President, I would like to say that I think it is a sad fact that one of the few people present today who have come correctly attired – and even wearing an LCC tie – in accordance with club rules, should be the lady who spoke earlier.'

The motion was carried by a seven per cent majority and the meeting was closed. That evening, my victory made the TV news and virtually every newspaper (including the 'quality' press) featured the story the next day. For once I was proud of the achievement that had led to this round of publicity.

12
REFLECTIONS

They say that God moves in mysterious ways and, having led such a very unusual life, perhaps I have more reason to believe that than most. Certainly the most recent event in my life has had the most unexpected consequences.

However, before I bring my story up to date, let me illustrate how truly remarkable the consequences of this event were by relating the attempts that David and I have made to effect a reconciliation with my parents. In December 1986 he telephoned them in the hope of being able to change their minds about seeing me. Subsequently my father wrote to David, attempting to explain what an impossibility this would be:

... I find it hard to marshall my thoughts to present them in a way that would help you to understand how my wife and I feel about our son's behaviour. He has been disfellowshipped from the organization of Jehovah's Witnesses and he well knows what this means and involves. We cannot compromize our faith and we are convinced that he would not expect us to. If you care to read the words recorded at Math. 10:37 you will see that we have no choice in the matter if we wish to follow the Christian way of life. We are not at liberty to pick out the parts that suit us and ignore the difficult parts, for as the Bible tells us at Ephe. 5:17 we must go on perceiving what the will of Jehovah is.

We loved our son dearly, and naturally we miss him very much. He however has chosen his way of life just as we have, but alas, they go in different directions. The only consolation that we have left is that he seems to have found happiness in his chosen way.

We hope, before it is too late, that circumstances will change. We send our Christian love to you all and remain....

Still I refused to give up hope.

In August 1988, having long wanted to show David where I grew up, we decided to spend a weekend visiting my old home town. As I had every intention of taking David to meet Auntie Elsie, I sent my parents a telemessage informing them that we would be staying at the Harpenden Moat House Hotel for the weekend – so that they wouldn't think we were doing something behind their backs when Auntie Elsie told them of our visit. Though I didn't really expect them to contact me, part of me secretly hoped that the very fact that we were so near might cause them to relent.

On Saturday morning I walked out to our car alone, while David went back upstairs for something he had forgotten. It was a beautiful, hot, sunny day, and while I wandered around admiring the flowers I was vaguely aware of an elderly lady climbing out of a car that had just pulled up. Then a voice behind me said: 'Stephanie?'

I turned around, and there in front of me was Mum. I hadn't recognized her because her hair, which had once been so dark, was now a pure snowy white! She was also much smaller than I had remembered. For a few moments we just stared at one another in disbelief. Then we flew into one another's arms and hugged each other, with tears pouring down our cheeks.

When David arrived he was totally nonplussed to be greeted by the sight of me holding on to this complete stranger's hand.

'This is my Mum, David.' I was so proud and excited I was grinning from ear to ear.

Over coffee, Mum explained how she'd just had to come down to explain in person why she and Dad couldn't have anything to do with me. She so wanted me to know that it had nothing to do with me and everything to do with the faith. When she told us that she'd not only defied Dad, who hadn't wanted her to come along, but had actually *told* him that she was going to defy him, I could hardly believe my ears. I hadn't thought I would ever live to see that day! It was a bitter-sweet reunion. Nothing had changed, but I was overcome with emotion at having seen Mum – and amazed by the bravery and determination she'd shown by actually coming to explain her reasons to us.

When Mum left I took David on a tour of Harpenden, pointing out the wood where I had played as a boy and the houses where all my old friends and acquaintances had lived. We even drove up my parents' street so that I could show David the house in which I had grown up and where my parents still lived. How I cried when I realized that we were so very near, yet still so far. That afternoon we visited my dear Auntie Elsie who, as always, welcomed us with open arms. And poor David had to watch as the tears started to flow all over again.

As we drove back north I turned to David and said: 'I'm not going to give up, David. We'll try again next year. We'll come back, and this time we'll invite Mum, Dad and Auntie Elsie to tea at the Moat House. And though Dad definitely won't come, who knows – Auntie Elsie and Mum might.' Clinging doggedly to that hope, I started writing little newsy letters to Mum and Dad. My firm belief that the maternal instinct was far, far stronger than anything else was rewarded when Mum began to write back.

Throughout 1989 and 1990 we continued working hard to expand our business interests. We set up a video production company in order to make our own specialist videos and thus be less reliant on the ones we had to purchase from importers. We launched TMC printing and copying shops, and JWA, our own advertising agency and design studio; we expanded the supermarket chain, and then immediately started making plans for our first Transformation branch overseas. The pace and the workload were killing. We scarcely ever went out because we rarely got home before nine or ten at night. And the harder we worked, the more I began to long for a little place in the country.

The idea of having a weekend retreat appealed to us both so greatly that we resolved to turn our dream into reality. After several false starts we found the perfect place: an old farm cottage high in the hills of north Wales. The moment we set eyes on the cottage, which had been extended and modernized without losing any of its charm, we were so struck by the sense of peace and tranquillity surrounding it that we knew it was the perfect place in which to recover from our increasingly stressful working week. In the event, our cottage turned out to be one of the most timely purchases we have ever made. For two months later, what initially seemed like a disaster struck us without any warning at all.

We'd just returned from spending a much-needed weekend at the cottage after suffering one of the worst weeks I had experienced in years. With Raiko working away at our latest Transformation shop in Newcastle-upon-Tyne for eight weeks, and David's recent acquisition of two more supermarkets, I had been left to cope single-handedly with a major computer crash which threw us into one of the biggest crises we'd ever had to deal with.

At the same time Domino, one of our beloved family of cats which by now numbered five, had ripped out her stitches following an operation and was in such a pitiful, distressed state that I had to give her round-the-clock nursing. I've always looked upon Sheba and the cats as my 'children' and though I loved them all equally, as a kitten Domino was particularly special. What with all the worry of the computer crash and its potentially disastrous consequences, and Domino, who cried piteously every time I tried to put her on the ground, I'd managed only three hours' sleep in three days. As if that wasn't bad enough, I'd been suffering a debilitating viral infection for several weeks.

'Thank God that week's over,' I said to David as I crawled thankfully into bed on Sunday night. Ten minutes later I began to feel extremely hot. I started to get out of bed, and then apparently crumpled to the floor in an unconscious heap.

When I regained consciousness some time later it was to find myself strapped to an ECG machine, surrounded by an ambulance crew and without any feeling at all in the right side of my body. David was hovering at my side. I thought I was going to die.

'Don't let them take me away,' I begged. 'If I'm going to die, let me die at home with you and the animals around me.'

I was so distraught that they had to call out my own GP who, after examining me, allowed me to remain at home. The following day he called round three times and, though I had regained some of the feeling in my arm, the fact that I couldn't co-ordinate my limbs and was also now experiencing problems with my eye gave him sufficient cause to recommend hospital. Though nobody had mentioned the word, we all thought I had suffered a stroke. In fact by the time I left Crumpsall Hospital ten days later everyone was convinced that I'd had a haemoplegic migraine, which apparently presents exactly the same symptoms as a stroke but doesn't have the same lasting effect.

For the first three or four days in hospital I was so weak I could hardly do anything for myself. But the one thing I was absolutely determined *not* to do was to suffer the indignity of using a bedpan. Because I insisted on going to the loo alone while in such a weak state of health my frequent pauses for rest on the other patients' beds along the way at least ensured that I got to know everybody well. If I had any concern about the reactions of the patients and staff when they discovered who I was, they were soon dispelled. Every single member of the staff and all my fellow patients were wonderful to me.

When such things happen, one is always tempted to feel sorry for oneself and ask, 'Why me?' If any such self-centred thoughts occurred to me, they were very speedily dealt with when I came to know Winnie, the sweet seventy-four-year-old lady who occupied the bed next to mine.

Winnie has motor neurone disease. In just 13 months she went from being a lively old lady who still loved to dance to a frail, wheelchair-bound shadow of her former self who can no longer walk, talk, move or swallow and has to be fed through a tube that is permanently taped to her nose. An electronic typewriter with a visual display unit was Winnie's only means of communication, and even that was a slow, tedious and painstaking process for her weak, shrunken frame. Just a few moments with Winnie were enough to teach me the sheer folly of self-pity when there are so many other people in this world who are worse off than ourselves. It's Winnie I have to thank for making me realize that love, affection and time are far more valuable and important gifts than anything else in life. She also taught me that you should voice your love while you can, for who knows what tomorrow might bring?

The second – and most amazing – thing that occurred as a direct result of my illness was that at long, long last I finally saw both my Mum and my Dad! Having waited until he knew that I was going to be all right, David had telephoned my parents to tell them I was in hospital. When he told me that the first thing they had said was that they wanted to come to Manchester to see me I could hardly believe my ears. David had arranged to drive down to collect them, but an unexpected snowstorm blocked the motorways and the journey had to be postponed. I shed tears when Mum spoke to me on the phone, and when I heard Dad's voice for the first time in so many years the lump in my throat was so huge I thought I would choke.

'Don't worry,' David told me. 'Now they've actually *said* they want to see you, I can't imagine anything keeping them away.'

A few days after being allowed home I went to the cottage to convalesce. I knew I had been given a warning, and it wasn't one I was about to ignore. Having come so close to losing my life, I couldn't help but realize how tenuous our grip on it is. My workaholic lifestyle had to change – there were more important priorities in my life now.

And one of those was making my peace with my parents. On the day of their arrival, David was up at four-thirty in the morning and on the road by five. I was still weak, so I couldn't bustle around like I might ordinarily have been tempted to do in my nervousness. Throughout the morning I kept wondering whether this was really such a good idea after all, reminding myself that it could quite easily go horribly wrong just as it had before. By the time they arrived, an hour earlier than expected and with me still unprepared, I felt like a nervous wreck.

The moment I opened the front door, Mum threw her arms around me and hugged me tight. For several seconds I looked at Dad. Physically he had hardly changed at all. Naturally he was a little bit older and a little more stooped, but I would have recognized him anywhere. Having no wish to embarrass Dad, I shook him by the hand. It took time for us all to relax, but gradually the conversation became less hesitant and stilted, and by the time we sat down to dinner that evening I knew that it was going to be all right.

There was one awkward moment at dinner when David started eating, only to be pulled up short by my father's voice calmly saying: 'Shall we just ask a blessing?' If ever a grown man could contrive to look like a naughty, scolded schoolboy, David did then.

The following morning Mum and I went for a walk alone together across the fields.

'I've been so afraid something might happen to you or Dad and I would never see you again. It never occurred to me that it could possibly happen to *me.*'

'Stephanie,' Mum said. 'We both love you. It's only because you've been disfellowshipped that we find it so difficult to see you now.'

'But if I had done something terribly wrong I could understand that,' I pleaded. 'It's such a tragedy. Why should I be excluded when I know of another trans-sexual who is a Jehovah's Witness like me and yet she has not been disfellowshipped?'

Mum could only shake her head sadly and sigh. No matter how much I tried to explain that mine was a recognized medical condition and I had merely had the recommended form of treatment, I knew she would never truly understand. And yet I knew that she did love me, and I understood what she was going through. For forty years my parents' entire life had revolved around their faith – a faith that they believed was being put to the ultimate test by their very own child! If my parents gave in now, they would be failing God. If they didn't give in, they would be failing me. What a terrible conflict they have had to face!

We turned back towards the house and Mum took my hand in hers. 'You know, it does our hearts good to see how happy you are.'

'I couldn't have a better husband than David,' I answered simply.

Although we tried to delay their departure as long as possible by taking them for a drive through some of the most spectacular scenery in Wales, eventually they had to leave. Mum and I clung on to one another in tears. Then I helped Dad into the car. When I had handed his sticks in to him and made sure he was comfortable, I was seized by an impulse to hug him and kiss him on the cheek. As I did so, Dad's hand gripped mine and, looking up at me, he said: 'We've really enjoyed seeing you, dear. Stay well.'

As David drove my parents away, I smiled despite the tears because for the first time in my life I understood what my father was trying to say. As a man who had been schooled to hide his emotions Dad couldn't possibly bring himself to say the words, but I had heard them anyway.

My parents and I have made our peace. But the problem has not been solved. Will I ever see them again? I don't know. They have written to me twice since then, and I sincerely hope they will continue to stay in touch. More than that I cannot say. Time has proved once that I was right not to give up hope. If I hold on to that hope, who knows what tomorrow might bring?

Time may heal many things, but the one thing time has not yet accomplished is a lessening of the grief and loss I still feel at having lost my children. In the seven years that have passed since I last saw Stephen, Andrew and Rebecca I have thought about them constantly, and I never give up hope that I might see them, too, again one day. I still treasure the letters they wrote to me before the awful publicity surrounding me forced us apart. When I look at Rebecca's girlish scrawl, it's hard to believe that my beautiful little girl is a woman of twenty now and already a part-trained accountant, or that Stephen and Andrew are twenty-two.

Although it has always been my dearest wish that we could all be reunited one day, I have to accept that that may never happen. Sometimes I wonder whether they ever think of me, but not knowing *what* they think about me is hard for me to cope with. I know their lives must have been very difficult, and when I reread Stephen's and Andrew's old letters I can only begin to imagine what they must have suffered because of who and what their father is. Phrases like: 'Rebecca told us that when Nanny found some of Mum's underwear in the wash, Great Nanny accused me and Andrew of having been wearing it...' in one of Stephen's letters to me still have the power to make me weep. Have their minds and lives been blighted forever by the prejudices of other people? Or have they found a way to come to terms with what was thrust upon them? If only they could know how I feel about them and how very much I want to reach out to them and hold them in my arms again.

But I can't. I'm wise enough to acknowledge that it's not for me to thrust myself into my children's lives – I can only wait, and hope and pray that one day they might find their way back to me.

Marylin and I have been in contact for some years now and, though it's unlikely we will ever meet, we spend long hours chatting on the telephone every few months or so. In the last few years I have been able to demonstrate to her that, if ever she or the children are in financial need, David and I will *always* be here. I'd like to be able to give my family much more than mere money, but as they haven't yet indicated that they would welcome more from me, for now I must be grateful that they allow me to meet even that need. But I will never give up hope that some day things might change.

I have no illusions about myself. I know that for the rest of my life I will be rejected, ridiculed and persecuted as a freak. To be a trans-sexual is not a solution – it is a last resort. If I had a choice I would far rather have been a complete husband to Marylin and a father to my own children – or a complete wife to David and the mother of his children. As it is, I never have been – and never will be – capable of totally fulfilling either role. I can be a stepmother to David's children – but, dearly as I love them, they will never be able to replace my own.

And yet, despite everything I would not wish the past undone, because the single – and the most brilliant – achievement of my life will, for me, always be that I fathered three children who are a credit to the world. Whatever they think of me, regardless of whether they ever accept me or not, I know that there is a part of me in them, and that makes me happy. I would never want to deny the love I feel for them, or the love I felt for Marylin. Perhaps that's why, if I have one regret, it is those two years of hell I put my family through at the end. If I had had the courage to walk away from them before that point I might have been able to spare them the worst of the heartache and pain. But I cannot undo what has been done, and if they cannot forgive me for what I have done, then I have to accept that.

When one is young, life is either black or white – it's only when you grow older that you become aware of shades of grey. To my children I am a memory that has possibly been overshadowed by other people's attitudes and prejudices. The only way I can ever hope to counteract that is by telling the truth – and that is what I have done.

In the meantime, I have found happiness and contentment. And that probably makes me unique amongst trans-sexuals, as so few of us have been fortunate enough to achieve fulfilment in *every* area of our lives.

The current UK laws relating to trans-sexualism are ridiculously archaic, and it is time they were changed. Unfortunately, trans-sexuals are such a small minority group that it's hardly in anyone's interest to bother. What seems so ridiculous is that you only have to look at me to know that I am a woman. Yet if I am convicted of breaking the law, as a legal male I would be confined to a men's prison with all its attendant horrors. My driving licence, my bank account and my credit cards are all in the name of Stephanie Anne Lloyd – and whilst I can register myself as Miss Lloyd, Ms Lloyd and even Stephanie Booth on my passport, I am forbidden to use the title 'Mrs' because my marriage to David is not legally recognized in Britain. That, in itself, highlights a ridiculous situation: because if I'm still legally considered a male, there is nothing to prevent me from marrying a female here. On the other hand, if I did, the moment I stepped outside the UK I could be prosecuted for bigamy as I'm legally married to David abroad!

If I 'can't be a woman because I can't have children', as one person pointed out to me during a TV interview, does this mean that all women who are infertile or post-menopausal are not women either? If I can't be a woman 'because I do not have a womb', does this bar all women who have had hysterectomies from being women? Of one thing I can be certain, I am most definitely *not* a man; and if I cannot be classified as a woman either, then what am I? A non-person?

I hope I have demonstrated in some small way how ridiculous current British law is. In years to come, I hope I will be able to challenge these laws and by so doing be instrumental in their change. Of one thing the world can be sure: the methods I shall use will not be conventional ones. At the same time I will continue to fight intolerance and prejudice with the most effective weapon I have: myself, because I do believe that people could learn from my experience.

Because I have been so fortunate, I would like to use the knowledge and the experience I have gained in future books to help others. I have experienced life as a man and a woman, a husband and a wife, a father and a stepmother and as both a son and a daughter-in-law. Those experiences have given me a unique and exciting perspective on life, love and relationships which I believe could be of benefit to everyone. I shall continue to see Winnie, who taught me that life is so precious we should never take it for granted, and I will continue to do what I can for those who are less fortunate than myself.

As for the future? Well, having lived such an unusual and controversial life, I cannot imagine that I shall stop doing so now. There is much yet to accomplish. And though I may never realize my ultimate dream to have my Mum and Dad, my three children and Marylin in my life again, I am as content as it is possible to be without these dreams. Facing death on two occasions has dramatically brought home to me the importance of genuine love and friendship. I have for my family David, whose enduring love, support and strength have made me happier and more fulfilled than I would ever have believed possible; my best friend Raiko, who is more like a brother to me; his mother Christine, who treats me as a daughter; Kevin and Sheila, who have proved to be such genuine and enduring friends; and David's wonderful parents and children; as well as Sheba and my beloved five cats to lavish my love and affection on. Is it any wonder that I feel moved to say: is there truly anyone more fortunate than I?